HOSTAGE TO HISTORY

Travels in Moldova

by

AKHIL BAKSHI

HOSTAGE TO HISTORY
Travels in Moldova

Publisher

Akhil Bakshi

Tower B-5, Flat 901, World Spa

Sector 30, Gurgaon (Haryana)

India

First Edition 2018

Type set in 11 pt Agaramond

Layout and typesetting by Swastik Printers, Gurgaon, India

Printed and bound by Swastik Printers, New Delhi, India

ISBN: 978-93-5321-975-8

A born tramp in love with wild places, Akhil Bakshi has been vagabonding around the world since his early years, finding telling beauty everywhere. He has led four major international motoring expeditions that have furthered the cause of peace and development. Vice President of the Indian Mountaineering Foundation, Fellow of the Royal Geographical Society, International Fellow of Explorer's Club, he is on the board of several adventure and sports organization's in India. He has founded two non-government organizations that work with rural youth and with small farmers and landless labour.

Akhil Bakshi has produced seventy television documentaries. Besides several e-books, his published books include: *The Road to Freedom; Silk Road on Wheels; Between Heaven and Hell; Back to Gondwanaland; I'll Follow the Sun, Arctic to Antarctic,* and *Askar Akaev- A Political Journey*

Atheism was the religion of the Soviet communists. Its ideology was to ensure extinction of existing religions, eliminate the possibility of conception of future religious dogmas, and impose its own doctrines and rituals. Like the vigorous worldwide conversions promoted, and often imposed, by the Christians - and the aggressive wholesale conversions conducted "at the point of the sword" by the leaders of Islam, the communists forced the masses to convert to their atheist tenets. Atheism, the new faith, would protect the exploited working class from the nefarious designs of the bourgeoisie that used religion - Judaism, Christianity, Islam or Buddhism - to suppress, enslave and control them. Once the Russian monarchy, devoted supporters of the Russian Orthodox Church, was replaced by the Bolsheviks in 1922, the communists, after having settled in, went hammer and tongs after the clergy and believers. Several bishops and thousands of priests were killed, and churches and mosques either destroyed or put to other uses. The church owned a significant chunk of Russia's real estate - to the chagrin of the suppressed serfs who, though greatly religious, backed the Russian Revolution. Its properties were confiscated, and a gag order placed on any public pronouncement. Though organised religion was never outlawed, believers were persecuted, and public worship discouraged. Pervasive propaganda in schools and mass media promoted science over religious superstition till reverence to a spiritual faith became a communal disgrace.

At the time of the Russian Revolution in 1917, there were about 54,000 churches in Tsarist Russia. By 1941, only 500 remained. The Nazi invasion of the Soviet Union in 1941, forced Stalin to suspend his anti-religion campaign and seek the support of the Russian Orthodox Church that experienced a brief revival. By the time Nikita Khrushchev became the Premier in 1958, 22,000 churches had been reopened. Religious publications could be circulated, and church membership expanded. However, an anti-religion campaign launched by Khrushchev saw Russian Orthodox churches dwindle to 7,000. Leaders of the clergy were jailed and substituted by pliable priests or KGB agents who propagated the state policy - and even furthered the "russification" of non-Russian Christians such as Orthodox Belarusians and Ukrainians. The leaders of the nationalistic Ukrainian Autocephalous Orthodox Church and the Belarusian Autocephalous Orthodox Church, that raised their heads under German occupation hoping for restoration of their power, were killed or sent to mental hospitals and labour camps in Siberia. Most of the 5,000 Jewish synagogues that existed before the Russian Revolution were shut down by Stalin and Khrushchev - leading to an exodus of Jews from the Soviet Union. Religious revival began, in small steps, with Gorbachev's glasnost and perestroika policies.

On a bright, sunny morning during the Easter week of 2018, while walking on Stefan cel Mare Avenue in Chisinau, Moldova's capital, Ioana pointed from afar the Transfiguration Church that shared its boundary with an imposing police security building that was once the former Soviet republic's KGB headquarter. "Let's not get too close. The police guards get nervous when they see tourists with cameras," advised Ioana. Disregarding her advice, I walked into the empty church with lavish interiors that are the hallmark of Russian orthodox churches. Consecrated in 1902, it had been transformed into a planetarium by the Soviets in 1962 during the Space Race period. Destroyed by fire in 1990, its ruins were handed over to the church that, after disintegration of USSR and Moldova's formal independence in 1991, lovingly renovated it with public funding.

"Easter was celebrated here yesterday – on April 7, a week after other Christian sects. My parents were diehard communists. Never believed in religion. We had no place of worship at home. After independence religion was back in vogue. Closed churches were reopened and church life revived. After decades of living under communist rule, people were hungry for religion. There were mass baptisms. Even old people wanted to be baptised. My father, a historian who develops museums, was an alcoholic. A friend of his suggested that he too should get baptised - just for fun. He did. And ever since that day, he has not tasted a drop of liquor. My mother, of Russian paternity, and a Romanian teacher, impressed by her husband's reformation, also became an ardent fan of the church," said Ioana.

"And your earlier generations? Did they also belong to the orthodox church?" I asked.

"We do not know much about our ancestors. All records were destroyed during the Second World War. All I know is: my maternal grandmother was a doctor."

"And your neighbours? Did they worship secretly?"

"Not that I know of. People feared someone ratting on them. I am glad the repressive communist days are over. Now the youngsters are looking westwards and have no love for the Russians. However, our Russian-educated and trained politicians are not on the same wavelength."

As we retraced our steps, to our left was a multi-storied, out-sized Presidential Palace under rapid construction. On the opposite side of the road was the national parliament. "Around this time in 2009, when the ruling communist party won the parliamentary elections, thousands of protesting youth gathered here. They feared that the leadership would steer the country towards Russia. Picking up the tiles we are walking on, they smashed windows of the parliament house, stormed it, ransacked the offices and set fire to the furniture. No one knows who incited the violence. We do not want to fall into Russia's lap again. The young prefer the freedom-loving culture of the west."Two boyish guards were on duty outside the parliament - and they were sniffing on something.

Youngsters have left Moldova in hordes to seek employment in western Europe. In 1991 there were 4.3million people in the country. Now there could be less than three million left (including the 300,000 in breakaway Transdniestria, a region controlled by Russian-backed separatists). The share of old people and children in the population is increasing and the workforce is shrinking.Money sent back home from workers abroad accounts for 25% of the country's annual income. A young couple, walking their infant in a pram, immersed in deep conversation, brushed past us. "I can imagine what they are talking about: whether to stay in Moldova or move westwards," said Ioana, grinning.

"Are you also planning to move?" I asked.

"I made several bad decisions with boyfriends. Been now with Steve, a real estate developer from Brisbane, for five years. We plan to marry and have a family in a year or two. I will move to Australia. That's where the wedding will be. I will fly my parents there. If I marry in Moldova I will have to shell out the money. It will be cheaper to fly just my parents to Brisbane. Most of my relatives are anyway in Italy, Germany, Spain, Holland and other parts of western Europe," she replied, lowering her voice.

Ioana works for seven months as a guide in Chisinau, moves to Australia in December and January when it is low season in Moldova and travels the world with Steve for another two or three months. She has been to 46 countries. Steve's favourite country is India. He finds the contrasts of wealth and poverty "awesome".

Until recently, Moldova received about 11,000 tourists a year. Only Tuvalu got fewer tourists. Aggressive tourism promotion has resulted in the numbers multiplying. Yet, the immigration officials are anything but welcoming. Earlier in the day, when I disembarked in Chisinau from the Aeroflot flight from Moscow that had skirted around Ukraine due to the existing political animosity between Russia and Ukraine, adding an hour of flying time, I had opted for the immigration counter manned by a young uniformed lady, plump and red-cheeked, with light-blue eyes and a face that had an ineffable charm. I respectfully presented her my passport and the e-visa. She read the passport from cover to cover with an attentive air, showing no concern for the passengers waiting behind me in the queue. I was following all her movements with my eyes and a pounding heart. Five minutes stretched to ten and fifteen – till the irritated passengers awaiting their turn, shook their heads and dispersed to other counters. I was the only one left in the hall. I asked her what the matter was, but she ignored me with bureaucratic coldness. Several times, with pricked ears, she tossed her gorgeous face towards the computer screen but couldn't resolve the problem. Finally, she consulted her superior and stamped me in. "And now you have a beautiful blonde guide as a compensation. Count your blessings," laughed Ioana when I narrated the episode.

Small, poor and distant, Moldova is known as the "butt-hole of Europe". The average monthly income is $300 – not enough to make a living in a town where a two-bedroom apartment rents for $250 a month. Most people have multiple jobs and live in joint families sharing the costs.

"Some of the elders, including my parents, are still nostalgic about the communist period. Assured jobs. Free accommodation, education, health care and gas. No worries. They had some money – but nothing to spend it on," said Ioana, sighing deeply.

With the political dissolution of the Soviet Union in 1991, economic disintegration followed. Rouble, the common currency of the republics, collapsed – and with it the savings of the people. "My parents had a life-time savings of 27,000 roubles. At that time, the rouble was on par with the dollar. For them it was a substantial amount. At independence, with the break-up of the Soviet Union, it was worth nothing. I was a child but still remember those difficult times. We really had to tighten our belts," mused Ioana.

We walked past the National Opera building. The plush bars adjoining it were overflowing with guests who didn't seem to be suffering any economic distress. A few steps ahead is the Triumphal Arch that commemorates the victory of the Russian Empire over the Ottoman Empire during the Russo-Turkish War of 1828-29 – that gave Czarist Russia a firm grasp over Moldova.

Moldova has also been the football of Europe. It has been kicked around more than any other place on the planet. During its rocky history it has been renamed, overrun, broken upand conquered countless times.

Though flint tools dating back to 800,000-1.2 million years have been found in Moldova, the region was the centre of the Cucuteni-Trypillia culture that lasted from 5500BC to 2750BC and stretched to parts of present-day Romania and Ukraine. The pastoral people later merged with the Dacians, an Indo-European tribe. Between the 1st and 7th centuries AD, the Roman and Byzantine Empires ruled the roost. Located strategically between Asia and Europe, fertile Moldova was invaded and ruled in later centuries by the East Germanic Goths, Central Asian Huns, nomadic Avars, Bulgarians, Magyars, Turkic Cumans, Mongols, Tartars, Poles, Lithuanians, Ottomans, Romanians and Russians.

Crossing a plaza decorated with gigantic Easter eggs, we entered the neoclassical Nativity Cathedral with a simple façade and opulent interiors. Bombed out in World War II, the communists destroyed its bell tower in 1962, and the Soviet authorities transformed into an exhibition centre. Originally built in 1836, the Chisinau's principal cathedral has three altars – Nativity of the Lord, the central altar; one dedicated to the patron saint John the New to the left; and to St. Martyr Nikita to the right. Among the many frescoes is one of Ștefan cel Mare, a king ordained with sainthood, and considered by the Molodovans as their founding father. He holds up the Christian Cross in this left hand – and a sword in the other hand.

During his long and stable reign of 47 years, Stefan made a reputation for himself as an astute politician and a skilled diplomat who played off the Ottoman Empire, Poland and Hungary against each other. He paid tribute to the Ottomans when it was advantageous and acknowledged King Casimir of Poland as his ruler when that seemed wise. When diplomacy failed, he resorted to arms. Of the 36 battles fought, he lost only two. He strengthened Moldovia by establishing an effective central administration, building new forts and restoring old ones. Peasants were obliged to bear arms. If a peasant was found unarmed or if he came to the army without spurs for the horse, he was pitilessly put to death. Such "reforms" enabled Stefan to greatly expand his forces. He institutionalised slavery and inflicted the harshest punishments, including impalement. If a folk legend is to be believed, he sacrificed gypsies to relieve Sulita of floods. In the 1470s, the crusading monarch fanned the persecution and extortion of Jews, Hussites and Gregorian Armenians. He liberally distributed confiscated lands to the Church and to his loyal supporters and valiant soldiers who exhibited bravery in battle. He opened his coffers for building new churches; encouraged development of monasteries; commissioned paintings with religious themes; and had exquisite tombstones carved for his ancestors. All these feats earned Stefan sainthood. He was canonised in 1992 by the Romanian Orthodox Church and is venerated as a saint – *Stefan the Great and Holy.* He is a national hero and a cult figure both in Romania and Moldova. His monuments have risen all over; his crowned head is present on currency notes; villages, streets and stations bear his name; voluminous literary works, poems and musicals eulogise him – and some plead with him to rise from the grave and lead his country once again. "Stefan the Great is the symbol of Moldovan identity. All our political parties accept him as the founder of our nation," said Ioana. "Incidentally, he was installed on Moldova's throne by his cousin, Vlad the Impaler, the prince of Wallachia, whose reputation for cruelty inspired the vampirical character of Count Dracula in Bram Stoker's 1897 novel," added Ioana.

"Stefan was the ruler of Moldavia – a region that, at various times, between the 14th century and 1859, comprised of all of present-day Moldova and parts of Romania and Ukraine. In 1859, Moldavia united with the Wallachia to form Romania. After that we had various identities, names and masters - mostly Russian and Romanian – until 1939 when, under the short-lived Molotov-Ribbentrop Pact, the neutrality agreement between Nazi Germany and Soviet Union, Romania was forced to cede Moldovan region, then known as Bessarabia, to the Soviet Union – leading to the creation of Moldavian Soviet Socialist Republic. We took name the 'Moldova' only after independence from

Soviet Union in 1991," clarified Ioana. We had the entire church to ourselves – except for a solitary lady in a blue scarf who was making her supplications at the main altar with tears rolling down her anguished face.

"Why isn't there anybody in the church?" I asked Ioana.

"Because they are all at the pubs."

"Doesn't the church offer them wine? Moldovan wines are good, I am told."

"They are great. And we are exporting all of it. In Soviet days, the Russians would take our best wines. The surplus was distributed to other republics. But then came Gorbachev and uprooted all our vineyards as a part of his anti-alcoholism campaign in the 1980s. With disintegration of Soviet Union, our economy collapsed - but the wine industry revived. Russians, thirsty for our stuff, were again buying up all our stocks. But, in 2006, when we did not agree to their terms to resolve the conflict over Transnistria, Putin slapped an embargo on our wine. Millions of bottles that had been purchased were not paid for. The wine industry went into a slump. But with the Russian fondness for our wines, the embargo was relaxed a little - but was again renewed in 2013 when we signed an association agreement with the European Union. Since then our wineries have directed their efforts at the EU - and met with great success. The free-trade agreement also helps. Last year the weather was bad in the wine-making countries of western Europe. Their wine production fell to the lowest level in 60 years. Since Moldova had good weather, its wine exports to EU skyrocketed. Perhaps that's why there is a shortage of good wine in the churches and people are not coming," she laughed.

"Just joking!" she continued. "I think they are staying away because it is a beautiful, sunny day - after months of cold weather. Until last week it was freezing. We had been attacked by the Beast from the East – an Arctic blast from Eurasia. Even Rome was hit by an unusual snowstorm a few days ago. Scientists say that it was because the weather in the Arctic region was unusually warm this year. As a result, sea ice in Arctic region is at a record low. The warmer environment that this creates allows cold air from the north to stream south across Russia, Scandinavia, and over the European mainland.You have brought the warmth from India."

"It's already 40-degree Celsius where I live. Can go up to 47 or 48 in May."

"Now that would make me melt like Arctic ice," she grimaced.

We walked down a pedestrian street with cafes that had moved outdoors to allow people, who had been in the grip of a cold snap until last week, to thaw themselves.

At the end of the road was the tall Leninist Komsomol Monument with a bronze sculpture of a victorious girl standing on a granite column holding high a lit torch, her dress fluttering in the wind. At the base of the column, just below another sculpture of a boy and a girl standing amidst fallen soldiers, is a plaque that states: *"EroilorComsomolului Leninist"*. The monument, a work of Moldovan sculptor LazărDubinovschi, commemorates the sacrifices of the members of the Young Pioneers organisation who died fighting against the Nazis during World War II.

"It was obligatory to be a Young Pioneer. I was one too," said Ioana.

Young Pioneers (abbreviated from Vladimir Lenin All-Union Pioneer Organisation) was a mass organisation of Soviet kids between the age of nine and fifteen. A brain-child of Lenin's wife, Nadezhda

Krupskaya, it existed between 1922 and 1991, replacing the Boy Scouts movement and creatively adapting their motto of 'Be Prepared' to 'Always Prepared'. It worked under Komsomol, the youth wing of the Communist Party of the Soviet Union (CPSU).

"Just like religious people set up an altar at home, we, the Young Pioneers, were required to set aside a corner in our house where we placed anti-religion literature and posters," said Ioana. This was in keeping with the communist religion of state atheism. "In rural areas, where commitment to Orthodox religion was stronger, such directives were opposed by the people." Nevertheless, the membership of Young Pioneers grew from 161,000 in 1924 to 14 million in 1940 and would top 25 million by 1974.

During World War II, thousands of Young Pioneers, mere children, nine to fifteen years old, died fighting in battles against the Nazis. The frayed monument we were standing at, memorialised their sacrifices.

To our right was a yellow, single-storey colonial building. "That's the hospital I was born in," said Ioana.

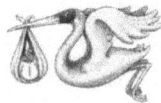

National Museum of Fine Arts, Chisinau

Transfiguration Church, Chisinau

Interior of Transfiguration Church, Chisinau

Interior of Transfiguration Church, Chisinau

Iconostasis of Transfiguration Church, Chisinau

Entrance and exit of Transfiguration Church, Chisinau

Facade of Transfiguration Church, Chisinau

PARLIAMENT HOUSE, CHISINAU

TRIUMPHAL ARCH, CHISINAU

NATIVITY CATHEDRAL, CHISINAU

INSIDE NATIVITY CATHEDRAL, CHISINAU

NATIVITY CATHEDRAL, CHISINAU

FRESCO OF STEFAN CEL MARE IN NATIVITY CATHEDRAL, CHISINAU

MONUMENT TO THE HEROES OF
KOMSOMOL, CHISINAU

On the front-side of the sprawling lawns of the hospital is the

Monument to the Victims of Jewish Ghetto. A tall, old man with a flowing beard holds the Torah in his right hand. On his heart is an overriding impression of a murderous left hand. "This entire area used to be the Jewish ghetto," explained Ioana. "During the Second World War, the Nazis and Romanians massacred their entire population. There is nothing left of the old ghetto. Some of it was destroyed in the 7.7 magnitude earthquake in 1940. The rest of it was levelled by German aerial attacks in 1941. This is also a memorial to the sad events of 1903."

The genocide against the Jews in western Europe is well documented and publicised. With Soviet clampdown on information, the wholesale extermination in Eastern Europe remained relatively unrecognised. It is only now, after the dissolution of USSR, that historians, accessing buried archives and sifting through dusty documents, are slowly bringing the macabre past to light.

As Bessarabia's importance grew as a trade route between the Black Sea and Poland in the 15th century, Jewish traders began settling the region. By the time Russia took control of Bessarabia in 1812, their population had grown to about 20,000 – andby 1897to 229,000 - accounting for 12% of the total population. Russia began persecuting Jews long before the Nazis. There were very few Jews living in Russia. Once Czarist Russia acquired huge swathes of territories with large Jewish populations in the Polish-Lithuanian Commonwealth between 1791 to 1835, that's when the hounding started. Jews were confined to designated areas called the 'Pale of Settlement' and prohibited from shifting to other parts of the Empire unless they converted to the state religion - the Russian Orthodox variety of Christianity. From 1821 onwards, pogroms - the deliberate persecution and violence against Jews approved or condoned by the Russian authorities - occurred on a regular basis, becoming successively bloodier.

In 1903, exactly 115 years ago, almost to the day I landed in Chisinau, during the Orthodox Easter holidays, the most horrific pogrom took place in the city. Earlier, a young Russian boy had been found murdered in Dubasari, a small town 37km from Chisinau; and girl who had committed suicide died in a Jewish hospital. Two slanderous anti-Semitic newspapers published reports insinuating that both the children were murdered as part of a Jewish ritual to use their blood for preparing *matzo*, the unleavened flatbread that is an essential part of the Passover festival. Though later investigation revealed that the boy had been killed by his own relative, the incited public unleashed a wave of violence against the Jews that lasted for three days. Forty-seven Jews were killed, hundreds wounded, 700 houses destroyed, countless women raped, and 2,000 families left homeless. The 5,000 soldiers stationed in the city did nothing to stop the rioting.

Abraham Polnovick, a Jewish eyewitness to the pogrom reported: *"Dead bodies were everywhere, many of them horribly mutilated, and in most cases with the clothes torn off. There were ears, fingers, noses lying on the pavements. Babies were tossed in the air to be caught on the points of spears and swords. Young girls were horribly mistreated before death came to end their torture."*

The New York Times reported: *"The anti-Jewish riotsin Kishinev, Bessarabia [modern Moldova], are worse than the censor will permit to publish. There was a well laid-out plan for the general massacre of Jews on the day following the Orthodox Easter. The mob was led by priests, and the general cry, "Kill the Jews", was taken up all over the city. The Jews were taken wholly unaware and were slaughtered like sheep. The dead number 120 [Note: the actual number of dead was 47–48] and the injured about 500. The scenes of horror attending this massacre are beyond description. Babies were literally torn to pieces by the frenzied and bloodthirsty mob. The local police made no attempt to check the reign of terror. At sunset the streets were piled with corpses and wounded. Those who could make their escape fled in terror, and the city is now practically deserted of Jews."*

The Russian ambassador to the United States, Count Arthur Cassini, dismissed this occurrence as a reaction of financially exploited peasants to Jewish creditors: *"The situation in Russia, so far as the Jews are concerned is just this: It is the peasant against the money-lender, and not the Russians against the Jews. There is no feeling against the Jew in Russia because of religion. It is as I have said — the Jew ruins the peasants, with the result that conflicts occur when the latter have lost all their worldly possessions and have nothing to live upon."*

Not all Jews were money-lenders. Most lived in poverty - working as farmers, cobblers, watchmakers, etc.

Two years later, in another pogrom, hundred more Jews were killed in Chisinau and other parts of Moldova.

The Chisinau incidents received widespread international publicity and were instrumental in spurring Jewish migration from the Russian empire at the turn of the 20th century.

When the Soviets reclaimed Moldova, then known as Bessarabia, in 1940, thousands of Jews suspected for disloyalty were sent to the *gulags*, the forced labour camps in Siberia.

Yet, when Nazis marched into Bessarabia, in 1941, Jews still accounted for half of Chisinau's population of 125,000. The Nazis annihilated them - butchering 53,000 of the city's 65,000 inhabitants.

"How did the Nazis kill them? Put them in gas chambers? Shoot them?" I asked Ioana.

"It was not just the Nazis. Also, the Romanians. Remember, Romania joined the Axis in late-1940. They were allies of the Germans and played a leading role in extermination of not only Jews but also the gypsies, the Roma people."

"But what were the methods they used?"

"First, they demarcated the boundaries of this ghetto, surrounded it with high wooden fence with only two entry and exit points. Jews could only leave the ghetto in groups and under military escort to work as forced labour on work sites. The handful of non-Jews who stayed on in the ghetto could move freely with special permits. Most of the wealthy Jews managed to escape by bribing the guards. It was the poor, living in buildings destroyed by German air raids, who were left behind to suffer their fate. This ghetto served mostly as a transit camp. Most of the Jews were taken across the Dniester River, in Transnistria, where you will be going tomorrow, and murdered. However, some massacres also took place here."

On August 1, 1941 a German lieutenant came to the Chisinau ghetto demanding 250 men and 200 women as labour for a work camp. Jews were assembled and the German officer, accompanied by three soldiers, made the selection, choosing mostly intellectuals and attractive women. He left with 450 Jews. In the evening of the same day 39 old Jews returned and narrated horrific stories of how the remaining 411 were shot near Visterniceni. The survivors were sent back only to report this event.

A few days later, a road inspector came to the ghetto and demanded 500 men to work at a construction site. The requested number was allocated to him, as well as an additional 25 women for cooking food. About a week later only 100 who were unable to work anymore returned, while the remaining 425 never came back.

On November 4, 1941, the Bessarabia newspaper reported: *"According to the available information, the last transport of Jews the other day left from Chisinau. As a result, the City Hall has started an inventory of the property of these Jews and those who left the city and went to Soviet Russia with the fleeing Bolsheviks. At the moment, a cataloguing of the abandoned Jewish goods is taking place. All goods will be stored and then sold to the public. Thus, thanks to the firm actions of Marshal, the capital of Bessarabia got rid of the Jewish leprosy that plagued Moldovans between the rivers Prut and Dniester for so long."*

Earlier, the same paper, on August 6, 1941, had applauded the ordinances issued by the military to establish the ghetto: *"Our Romanian Bessarabia, despite the horrible scars of national liberation war, is coming back to the mainstream of orderly life, such as it was before the June 28, 1940. Jews, destroying everything in their path, burning churches and institutions, fled with the Red Army to Moscow to Siberia, to the Urals and beyond. Opposed to civilization and the Heavens, opposed to the Christianity, these defilers of the icons finally took the masks off and demonstrated their true feelings and 'love' for the peaceful and patient Romanian people. They wanted to bring us to our knees, to make us their servants. But their time has passed. Now is the payback hour for the committed deeds! ... (The establishment of the ghetto) is necessary because the Jews stayed in Chisinau pursuing their usual criminal goals of weakening the foundations of our nation-state."*

The Jews of the Chisinau ghetto were sent on a 'death march' to the camps in Transnistria. The authorities did not expect all the undernourished, starving Jews to survive the exodus. General Topor, a Romanian, gave orders for the digging of a "grave every 10 kilometres for about 100 persons where those lagging the convoys will be gathered, shot and buried."

Those who made it to Transnistria were shot, hung, or burnt alive by being hounded into barracks that were set on fire. The dead bodies were thrown into mass graves. "Tomorrow, if you can, do visit the Tiraspol Jewish Cemetery. After the war many of the massacred Jews were reburied here in common graves. See the tombstone of Mira Vladimirovna Gershenzon. She was born in 1839 and died in 1965 – at the age of 126!" suggested Ioana.

Within one year, the Jewish population of Chisinau had been reduced from 65,000 to 86. By the time the Soviet Red Army reoccupied Chisinau in August 1944, it is believed the Nazis had liquidated about 300,000 Jews across Bucovina, Bessarabia and Transnistria.

Liberation after World War II turned into nearly five decades of communist oppression. In 1961, the Soviet government forbade Jews from observing Bat Mitzvah, their religious service. In 1964, all synagogues in Moldova were closed except one in Chisinau.

After independence, the Jewish culture is slowly re-emerging. Synagogues have reopened, and the Jewish population has grown to about 12,000 – mostly poor and elderly. While walking through the former ghetto, we came across two Jewish students in black suits, their curls swirling down their black hats, their families in tow, walking and talking joyously. Ioana engaged them in a conversation. They were Israeli students studying International Relations at the Moldova State

University and their parents and siblings had come to visit them from Tel Aviv during the Easter break.

MONUMENT TO THE VICTIMS OF JEWISH GHETTO, CHISINAU

The blazing sun was scorching my uncovered head. We crossed the road to take advantage of the shade. Ioana pointed out the modern building of National Bank of Moldova. "Our central bank with no money," giggled Ioana.

"Where has all the money gone?" I asked.

"Our politicians took it. Most of our leaders are moneybags. They have business interests. $1 billion was stolen from three banks through fraudulent loans and transfers. Everyone is involved – not just the politicians. Judges, prosecutors, regulators..." revealed Ioana.

"Wow! India, too, is currently reeling under a bank scam. A business family with political connections scammed a bank of $2 billion – the same way - and fled the country!" said I, interrupting her.

"Relative to the size of your economy, that is nothing. In our case, $1 billion is equivalent to an eighth of our GDP. Twelve percent of our GDP got stolen! That must make it the greatest bank fraud ever!" exclaimed Ioana.

"How did it affect you?" was my question.

"Its impact on the public was limited. Banks had no money to give loans – but since a third of our workers are small farmers who do not borrow from banks, this went largely unnoticed. Good weather led to 30% rise in grain production and farmers had more money in their pockets. This National Bank took over the insolvent banks and injected fresh capital into them by printing more money. This led to inflation. Leu, our national currency, weakened. So, the Moldovans working abroad sent more foreign exchange home – and got a good deal. Because of all these factors the adverse impact of the bank scam on the public got somewhat cushioned," explained Ioana. "Interest rates went up.

Investment declined. Government didn't have enough funds to pay its employees. No new welfare programmes could be undertaken. Old ones were curtailed. Two state hospitals in Chisinau had to close for a while. Only emergency services were available. And in the middle of all this our prime minister had to resign as he had forged his high school diploma," said an exasperated Ioana.

"Oh, my god! Moldova and India are so alike!" I exclaimed. "Even our prime minister is accused of forging his university degree. And the University of Delhi has told the court that it cannot release records pertaining to 1978, the year the prime minister claims he graduated. And who runs your country now?"

"The leader of opposition!"

"What?"

"This is seriously a strange country," laughed Ioana. "Vlad Plahotniuc is one of the richest men in our country. In the 2014 parliamentary election, his Democratic Party lost - getting only 16% of the vote. Yet, through his money power he controls over half the deputies in parliament – and hence the government. Most of the judges are in his pocket. Whoever opposes him gets into trouble. In 2016, Prime Minister Vlad Filat, who was his greatest political rival, was framed and dismissed for abusing his power. People like Igor Dodon, the current president, detest Plahotniuc. But some believe they are secretly working together. The president leans towards Russia. Plahotniuc projects himself as more pro-West. Recently, the president blocked the appointment of the defence minister proposed by government. This man favours closer cooperation with NATO and is also close to Plahotniuc. They had the constitutional court suspend the president for a couple of days so that the defence minister could be appointed. Ridiculous! So, we don't know which way we are going- whether with EU towards west or Russia towards the east. I guess we are just stuck between pro-Russian thieves and pro-EU thieves," sighed Ioana.

"Which way would you like to go?"

"I would like Moldova to be independent. Have good relations with both Russia and EU and not formally align with any of them," she replied, diplomatically.

We got back on Stefan cel Mare Boulevard, Chisinau's main thoroughfare, and walking past the imposing Government House headed slowly uphill towards the war memorial under a blistering sun. Stopping to browse handicrafts and memorabilia for sale at a small flea market, I picked up Lenin pins worn by communist party members and by Young Pioneers.

Like other Soviet republics, little Moldova, after being tossed around between Russia and Romania for two centuries, is trying its best to form its own national identity.In the 1980s, when Gorbachev introduced the policies of perestroika and glasnost, encouraging decentralisation and political liberalisation, there was an immediate awakening of nationalism amongst ethnic Moldovans. The Popular Front of Moldova was formed. In 1988 they demanded from the Soviet authorities that Moldovan, not Russian, be declared the state language; and the Latin script, rather than the Russian Cyrillic script, be used. The more radical elements wanted the minorities, mostly Slavs – that is, Russians and Ukrainians, expelled from Moldova. "On August 31, 1989, giving in to public pressure and in recognition of the shared Moldovan-Romanian linguistic identity, the Soviets accepted the language demands," explained Ioana.

"And we are crossing a street by that name – Strada 31 August 1989!" I observed, pointing at the road sign.

"Yes. I remember that day clearly. I went to school and the blackboard in class had something written in big letters in Romanian – and in Latin script. I was shocked!" she recalled.

Culturally threatened and fearing a possible integration of Moldova with Romania in the future, the ethnic minorities, the Russians, formed their own movement demanding equal status for Russian and Moldovan languages. However, in 1990, in the first free parliamentary elections held in Moldavian Soviet Socialist Republic, the nationalist Popular Front won – and began implementing their agenda. Both sides formed armed vigilante groups that attacked each other. In the Russian-dominated Transnistria, on the eastern bank of the Dniestr River, the people's representatives proclaimed the narrow valley as Pridnestrovian Moldavian Soviet Socialist Republic. Though it was not accepted by President Gorbachev, Soviet Union was already in a turmoil and too weak to enforce the decision. Slowly, the separatist government took control. Moldova declared its independence from the Soviet Union on August 27, 1991. Six months later war broke out between Moldova and Transnistria. The Russian army supported the separatists before brokering a ceasefire that has lasted until now, making it a 'frozen conflict'. Over 700 people died in the war. Though the Russians have established a military base in Transnistria, even they don't recognise it as an independent country.

"Is it Transnistria or Transdniestria?" I asked Ioana.

"It's the same thing. Transnistria is Romanian. Transdniestria is Russian. It's like saying Moskva instead of Moscow," she answered. "Language is a major issue between us. Moldovan and Romanian languages are the same. Transnistrian authorities have banned teaching in Romanian language in primary schools. Once, their paramilitary machine-gunned the Latin letters from a classroom wall. Our resistance to Russian is a reaction against the imposition of that language on us. Whenever we spoke in Romanian, the Russians would tell us to speak in a 'human language'. For two centuries we were told how inferior we are. They brainwashed us into believing that we were no good. If there were fifty Moldovans in a room talking in Romanian and a Russian came in, everyone would switch to talking in Russian."

"Are you closer to Romania or Russia?"

"Definitely Romania. We speak the same language. Have a shared history and traditions. Romania supplies us with energy, buys a big share of our exports. Many Moldovans have dual citizenship and work in Romania. But just because we have a shared culture it does not mean that we are a Romanian land. Even Austria and Germany have a common culture – but are different countries. Denmark, Sweden, Norway have a Viking past and a shared Scandinavian culture – but are independent countries. Moldova, as a state, appeared long before Romania, or even Wallachia, the Romanian Kingdom. Bessarabia, or Eastern Moldova, was given to the Russian empire in 1812. The western part of Moldova united with the Romanian kingdom, and later with Transylvania, and formed the country Romania. In 1918, on gaining independence from the Russian empire, Bessarabia became part of Romania – and remained so until 1940, when it was given to the USSR, due to the Ribbentrop-Molotov pact. I have told you that before. Moldova is NOT a part of Romania, even though most Romanians believe so."

"Do you think unification with Romania is a possibility?"

"Of course, we have many Moldovans who favour unification with Romania. Their arguments are that we are two Romanian states separated after Second World War when the conquering Soviets redrew the map of Romania. We should unite like East and West Germany. Romania's per capita income is four times higher than ours and uniting with them will bring prosperity – as well as direct entry into the EU of which Romania is already a member. A delay in uniting might bring us again under the Russian boot..."

A black granite plaque with a stone wreath placed over it announced Eternity Memorial Complex that honours the Soviet soldiers who died in the Second World War, fighting to liberate Moldova from the Nazis. The central memorial is a pyramid of five 25-metre tall bayonets cut from black and red granite. On the floor, sheltered by the bayonets, is the eternal flame. "Each of the pillars represents one year of the war fought from 1941 to 1945," remarked Ioana.

"But I thought the Second World War started in 1939," I mumbled.

"It did for the world. When Nazis attacked Czechoslovakia in 1939. At the time the Nazis and Soviets were partners in crime, merrily annexing countries. They both made a coordinated invasion of Poland, dismembering it. Soviet Union gobbled up Latvia, Lithuania, Estonia and Moldova. It was only when the Nazis attacked USSR in 1941 that the Great Patriotic War, as they call the Second World War, began for the Soviets," explained the knowledgeable guide.

She continued: "Moldova was one of the first countries to be attacked. Germany's plan, Operation Barbarossa, was to conquer western USSR, use the Poles and other Slavs as forced labour for the war effort, take-over the oil reserves of the Caucasus, and food resources of the Soviet republics. Moldova's role, as envisaged by the planners sitting in Moscow, was to produce vegetables and wine. We, as a republic of USSR, had not been allowed to industrialise. Romania allied with the Nazis and supplied their war machinery with oil."

"Did some Moldovans also support the Nazis?" I asked.

"The former aristocracy and big landlords who had suffered under the rule of the Bolsheviks were initially happy to see the Red Army ousted by the Germans – but soon discovered that the Nazis were as bad. My paternal grandfather, a landlord, was exiled by Stalin to Kazakhstan. That's where he first met his future wife – daughter of an exiled Ukrainian landlord."

A girl was skateboarding A father was pushing a pram with a child. A young couple was taking selfies. Other than them and us, the complex was vacant. A granite column with a massive bronze crown says, 'we have not forgotten you'.

"On our national days, this place is full. All of Chisinau walks here to lay flowers at the memorial. We have mountains of flowers here. It is strange that there is no soldier here today guarding the eternal flame. I have never seen this before," commented Ioana.

There were three old cemeteries at this site: Orthodox, Lutheran and Lipovan. The Heroes cemetery contains the graves of soldiers who fell during the Iasi-Chisinau Soviet offensive to liberate Moldova from the Nazis. A black cross marks the cemetery of the German soldiers.

"The liberation of Moldova in August-September 1944 was also a turning point in the war," said Ioana. "The Red Army encircled the German and Romanian forces near Chisinau, cut off their retreat, capturing 115,000 enemy soldiers. Romania, after a coup master-minded by their King Michael, dumped Germany and switched their allegiance to USSR and the Allies. Soon, the German armed forces were facing severe fuel shortages. This victory also paved the way for the Red Army to chase the Germans out of Yugoslavia and other parts of eastern Europe. It was only after the Soviet victories in Moldova and Romania that Hitler admitted, for the first time, that the war was lost."

While leaving the complex, Ioana pointed out the monument honouring Moldovan soldiers who died in the 1991-92 Transnistria War.

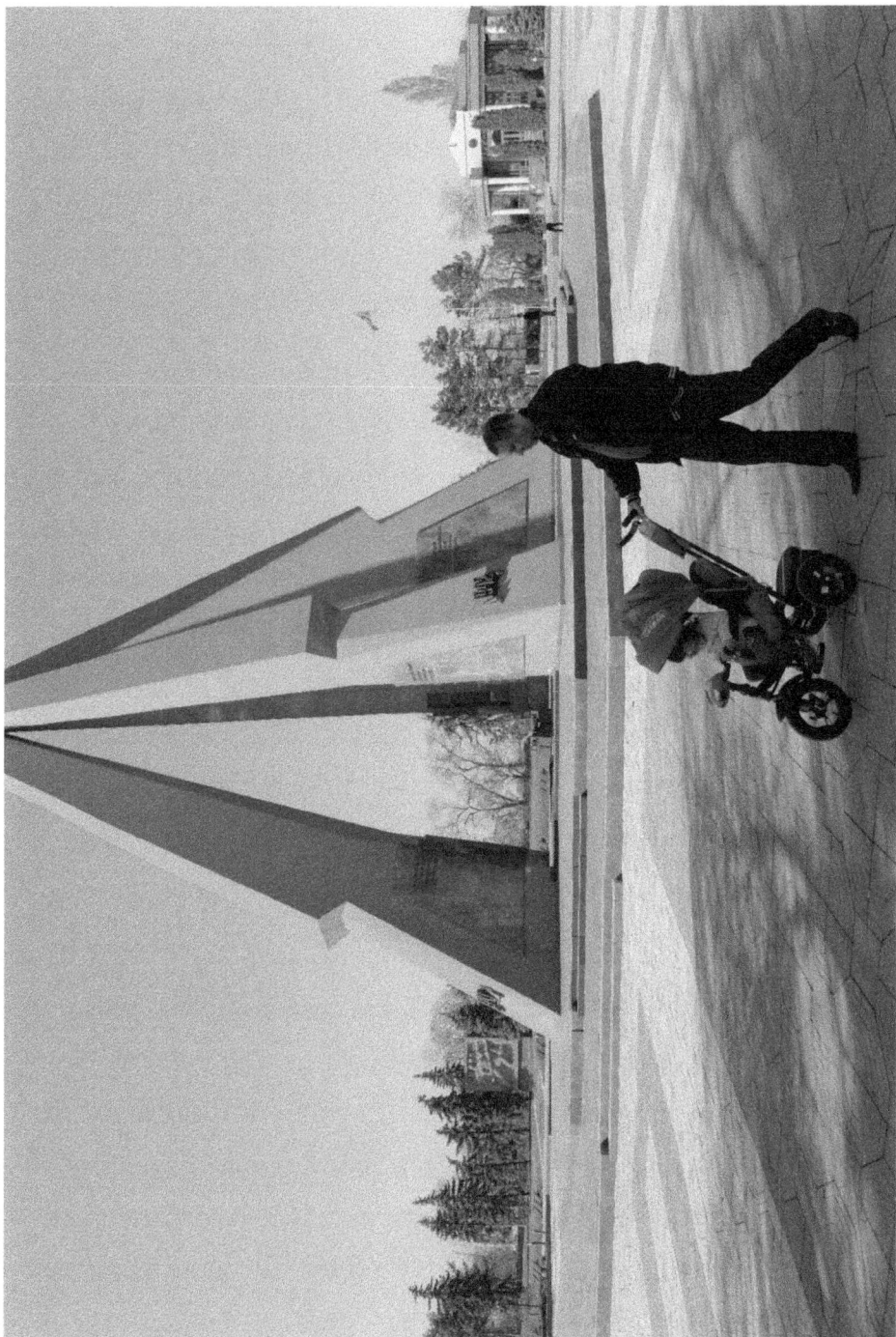

ETERNITATE MEMORIAL COMPLEX, CHISINAU

Walking towards the Ciuflea Monastery, Ioana, with a wave of her hand, drew my attention to the half-dozen incomplete buildings with idle cranes suspended over them. Some of the buildings displayed signs offering sale. "Either there are no buyers. Or the developers ran out of funds - or left the country," said Ioana. "But all is not so bleak. Moldova has one of the highest internet speeds in the world. Many companies have located their call centres here."

It was almost five in the evening by the time we got to Ciuflea Monastery aka St. Theodor Convent. In soft light its pastel blue and white walls supporting an array of lofty and short turrets crowned with golden onion domes, were very appealing to my camera. Ioana covered her head with a scarf before entering the convent. Its opulent interiors reeked of burning candles that signify spiritual purity and victory over darkness. They also provide income for the church. To the delight of the young priest with a striking beard, a bunch of elderly ladies, murmuring prayers, lit dozens of candles and placed them in holders that resembled giant pies. The walls were painted brightly with scenes from the Bible that provided, in old times, the visuals for the priest's sermons addressed to an illiterate public.

The frescoes in an Orthodox church follow a set pattern: the dome is reserved for Christ; scenes from the life of Jesus are depicted on the ceiling space between the dome and the walls; further down the wall are illustrations of Christ's final week on earth; and the ground-level portrays historical characters, kings and donors. In the nave, the main body of the church, there were no benches or seats – for one must stand before god. Following its roots in the Jewish tradition, men and women stand separately in the church – men on right, women on left.

A magnificent chandelier adorned with tall candles hung from the ceiling. We faced a giant golden wall richly ornamented with large, glorious icons. Ioana explained that this wall was a screen, called iconostasis, that separates the nave from the sanctuary where the altar, bishop's throne and chairs of the priests are placed. "At the centre of the screen is the 'Beautiful Gate' from where the priests enter the sanctuary. As you look straight at the screen, on the right is an icon of Christ, followed by an icon of John the Baptist. On the left of the gate is the icon of Theotokos, as Mary is known in Eastern Christianity, holding baby Jesus. All iconostasis in Orthodox churches follow the same pattern. Women are not allowed to enter the sanctuary, the area behind the iconostasis. Men can do so only if invited by the priest," clarified Ioana.

Consecrated in 1858, the monastery was financed by AnastasieCiufli, a Macedonian merchant who, along with his brother Teodor, had migrated to Bessarabia in 1821. In doing so, he fulfilled his brother's last wish – to have a church built in honour of his namesake, Saint Theodore of Amasea who, according to Christian mythology, was tortured and thrown into a furnace,around 406 AD, for opposing paganism. Later priests stretched Theodore's legend, attributing to him powers to influence the course of battles – that led to his becoming the patron saint of crusaders. The remains of both the merchant brothers are placed in the monastery. When the communists downed the shutters of Chisinau's principal church, the Nativity Cathedral, Moldova's high priest moved here, elevating the status of the monastery.

Beaten by the scorching sun, we hopped on a city bus and got off at the Opera House. Crossing the road, we walked past the imposing statue of Stefan the Great raised on a high pedestal, and entered the iron-fenced Pushkin Park, renamed Stefan cel Mare Central Park. Three Protestants had put up a stall near the entrance to introduce their brand of religion. As no one seemed to be interested, they gossiped amongst themselves. "Protestants and Baptists are campaigning very hard to get a share of the market. They put up stalls in public places – like parks and malls," remarked Ioana.

The park's nickname 'The Park of the Lovers' describes its function truthfully. Here and there, sitting on wooden benches under old and leafless acacia and mulberry trees, behind bushes and amongst emerging flowers, were young and old couples holding hands, locked in loving embrace, or stealing kisses. Kids ran amok chasing pigeons, playing hide and seek, or whizzing around on cycles or rented buggies. We walked through the Alley of Classics of Moldovan Literature, over the shadows cast by the tall trees, glancing at the glistening busts of famous Romanian and Moldovan writers and poets, perched on red granite pedestals, that seemed to come alive in the magical lushness.

"Originally, there were only twelve sculptures," said Ioana. "After independence we added a couple more of writers and poets who were banned during the Soviet period." All the paths in the 17-acre park lead to the central fountain, an exquisite work of art, that was emitting rainbows and welcome sprays of cold water.

Close to the fountain is the monument to the celebrated Russian author Alexander Sergeyevich Pushkin – a green bust placed on a tall granite column. Kicked out by the Czar, in 1820, for his liberal views and scandalous writings, Pushkin was exiled in Chisinau, then a distant outpost of the Russian empire, between 1820 and 1823. From the sunny Crimean coast, he rode into Chisinau and was immediately depressed by the town's narrow streets and small houses only few of which were built of stone. By and by, he found the city perfectly suited to his Bohemian ways.

The stunning Moldovan ladies, of mixed Turkish, Greek and European composition, until recently kept in harems according to the Turkish-Muslim culture, were experiencing freedom - attending balls and masquerades, reading erotic French novels, and generally seeking pleasure and entertainment. They were amorous and frivolous. As in Russia, the 22-year-old Pushkin succumbed to the world of vice and easy pleasures. Every beautiful girl or woman was fair game. He thoughtlessly flirted and had affairs with daughters and wives of landlords and generals, noblemen and commoners, friends and hosts. Several adulterous ladies got Pushkin into trouble with their husbands who would challenge him to a duel. Pushkin always took up the challenge and turned up for the fight. Sometimes the husbands would miss their mark and offer a compromise that was readily accepted by Pushkin. Most of the time, Pushkin's friends would settle with the aggrieved husbands.

It was probably here, in this 'park of lovers', that he was having a liaison with Ludmila Shekora, an ethnic Gypsy known for her beauty, when the boy appointed to keep a look-out for Inglezi, the lady's husband, reported that the suspecting spouse was walking hastily towards them. Both Ludmila and Pushkin ran in opposite directions. However, they had been seen together. Ludmila was placed under confinement. Pushkin was challenged to a duel that never took place – thanks to the intervention of his friends. The gypsy lady might have inspired Pushkin's masterpiece *Ruslan and Lyudmila*.

Pushkin had no qualms about sleeping with several women at the same time. Once, he was walking in a park with an aristocratic lady when another mate of his, a swarthy gypsy woman, hiding behind a bush, jumped on the lady, threw her on the ground and began to pulverise her face. Pushkin, unable to separate them, got hold of a stick and beat the gypsy who was about to pummel him next - but let him be. Many had witnessed this incident and it became the talk of the town, forcing an embarrassed Pushkin to remain indoors for a fortnight.

It was in Chisinau that Pushkin, when resting from his amorous intrigues, drunken bouts, gambling and frequent duels, wrote *The Prisoner of Caucasus*.

A group of old, boisterous men, unshaven, wearing Scottish Tartan-style caps and worn-out jackets, sat on a bench, talking loudly and spitting profusely. "These are those guys," said Ioana with a sneer and an altered voice.

"Which guys?'

"Those who want Moldova to join with Romania."

"How do you know?"

"From the way they dress and speak," she said, scowling.

Ioana dropped me at my sprawling hotel, Jolly Allen, bang opposite the park's parameter, where I seemed to be the only guest.

ST. THEODOR TIRON CONVENT, CHISINAU

INSIDE ST. THEODOR TIRON CONVENT

ST. THEODOR TIRON CONVENT, CHISINAU

Statue of Ştefan cel Mare
at the entrance of
Central Park

CENTRAL PARK, CHISINAU

To greet the morning sunbeams I woke up early, dressed, had a hasty breakfast and stepped out into **Stefan cel Mare Central Park** for a quick stroll before Alex came to drive me to Transnistria. It was a beautiful day, the sun's warmth soothing the top of the spindly trees that were breaking out with leaves under the comforting breath of spring. The fountain danced joyously. Chirpy birds flitted about looking for breakfast.

The young, lanky Alex was too serious for a guide. After passing high school, he trained in information technology but found profitable employment in driving and guiding tourists. Ioana had assured me that he had the necessary connections in Transnistria to ensure a hassle-free visit. Cops at the immigration post and in Tiraspol, the unrecognised country's capital, are known to rough-up tourists, slap false charges on them and release them only after their palms had been adequately greased. Alex would ensure that nothing like that happened to me. It took an eternity to cover the 60km distance to the border. The potholed, single-track road was lined on both sides with walnut trees glowing in the warming rays of early spring and preparing to welcome fresh crowns of whispering leaves. Deftly dodging potholes, Alex kept me entertained by spreading rumours about villainous Russians - stories that will only further the hereditary feud amongst the two communities.

Parking the car at the border, Alex asked me to hide my camera under the seat and follow him. I did as I was told and walked to the immigration office in dread. No courtesies can be expected from a whimsical cop. Through a small slit in a huge window of darkened glass, Alex presented my passport to the officer. Leafing through the document and giving me a murderous look, he barked some questions that were answered by Alex with a deference suited to the size of the cop's pompous hat. There is nothing cheerful about a communist official. Their social abilities could do with greater cultivation. Anyway, I got my 'coupon' to enter Transnistria. The passport was not stamped.

Driving slowly, we entered Bender, once known as Tighina, a small city on the west bank of Dniester River, located in the buffer zone established after the 1992 Transnistrian War – but under the administrative control of Transnistria. From afar we saw the red-turreted Bendery Fortress, originally built by Stefan cel Mare before being captured by Suleiman the Magnificent in 1538 and refurbished as an Ottoman structure. In early 19th century, it fell to the Russian troops who massacred every single Turkish Muslim they could lay their hands on. Until recently it had been a functioning Russian army base that has since moved to another site, a few kilometres south of the fortress.

We drove by the new Russian base, a fortress sunk in ground, its towering mud walls, formed by nature, hidden behind a thick growth of creepers. Calm reigns around the fortress. With no good insurrections, revolts or wars to attend to, the principal occupation of its resident soldiers is to keep the populace in obedience, harass innocent citizens and extort money from tourists - when they are not dressed up for drills and reviews. Several uniformed soldiers were striding along the fortress wall with extraordinary solemnity. Though military service is no burden to them, none looked happy. "Hardened drunkards," sneered Alex.

Alex parked in front of the Bender Memorial Arch, so I could take some pictures. Along with the humble Arch, I shot the imposing statue of Potemkin, the Russian general who captured Bender fortress from the Ottomans and was said to be the lover of Catherine the Great. Behind the statue was a monumental entrance to a cemetery. A big-hatted soldier was tranquilly having his lunch when he saw me walking toward the entrance. Brushing aside his plate, grinding his teeth, he marched towards me with long strides. Surely, he was going to hold me by the scruff of the neck and yank my ear for photographing the arch and the statue, I thought to myself. He waved his hands towards the cemetery, barking in Russian, repeating the same words. Ah! He wants me off the premises. Or is he delivering my funeral oration?

"DobreUtro!" said I with all possible coolness, trying to appear unflustered while trembling inside. I was prepared to accept my fault for photographing the monument, apologise for my unpardonable impudence, and, not knowing the language, plead innocence for not following the "No photography" sign - if there was any. Meanwhile, Alex came trotting towards us. The soldier shouted some words at him. "He wants you to go down and see the cemetery," smiled Alex. Even if a Russian soldier or cop is being helpful and friendly, there is nothing free and easy in his manner. Grimacing with glee, I shuffled away to meet the dead.

The manicured cemetery is stuffed with soldiers, friends and foes alike, who fell fighting for their country on the soil of Transnistria in the last 200 years – Russians, Swedes, French, Hungarians, Romanians and Soviet Moldovans. The Second World War accounts for 356 graves – 338 Romanian and 18 Soviet. "This cemetery honours all soldiers – even our enemies – who died for their country," said Alex. A grim reward for martial glory.

As we exited the necropolis, I glanced at the soldier, the custodian of the cemetery. He had finished his lunch and was washing the dishes.

On way to the old Bender railway station, Alex pointed out a mansion, probably the City Hall, whose white walls, lavishly pockmarked with bullet holes, showed signs of savage combat during the Transnistria

War. It was a sorrowful epitaph of past times. Inexperienced and unruly groups of fighters had rushed headlong into combat, butchering each other. In no time, outsiders stepped in. Russia, sympathetic to their Transnistrian brethren, armed the separatists. Romania provided weapons to Moldova. The nastiest period of the war was from March 2 to July 21, 1992. Both parties, drunk on enmity, but raw in the art of warfare, had gone on fighting amongst themselves without reaching a conclusion. With no sign of a swift and successful end, and dismayed by their own performance, the vicious rivals looked numbly upon Russia for intervention. Major General Alexander Lebed took over the Russia's 14th Army and went headlong into battle, obliterating Moldovan forces in Bender. However, he had no love for the separatist Transnistrians, denouncing them as bandits and criminals. "I told the hooligans in Tiraspol and the fascists in Chisinau – either you stop killing each other, or else I'll shoot the whole lot of you with my tanks," he is stated to have said. Yielding to Lebed's threat, the warriors unclenched their guns. Russia had forced the cessation of the tedious and petty war fought between brigands more than armies. The floundering, battle-weary combatants went back to their carefree slumber.

We got off the vehicle at spectral Bender railway station that was devoid of traffic and passengers. Even the ghosts seemed to have deserted it. Only stray dogs were loitering in the square opposite the charming station. But it was not always so. The first railway line was laid in the Transnistrian region in 1871. By 1917, Bender had 253 locomotives and was the biggest station on USSR's South-Western Railway. During the Great Patriotic War, or World War II, it was a frontline station transporting troops and weapons – thus attracting German air raids. An old Russian CY 06-71 steam locomotive and the adjacent granite mural memorialising the rail workers who lost their lives during the 1917 Russian Revolution are now the only remaining items of interest.

Alex stopped outside Gorky Cinema. Before he could tell me more about the structure, I darted across the road, Lenin Avenue, to Lenin Park to see Lenin's airy statue. I photographed it from all angles and had Alex take my pictures with the revolutionary leader's flamboyant statue in a majestic pose. "We had several statues of this fellow in Moldova – but we have demolished most of them. Whenever the authorities take down his statue, the communist supporters demand its restoration. Many times,they have re-erected his statue. We still have nine or ten of them," sniggered Alex.

Before crossing the Dniester River, Alex slowed down at a memorial park dedicated to the Transnistrian victims of the 1992 war and asked me if he should stop. Noticing his disdain for the Transnistrian cause, I preferred to continue to Tiraspol. While crossing the bridge, an angelic lady dressed in a miniature bikini bicycled past us. A visibly aroused Alex latched on to her tail and followed her closely, his eyes popping out of their sockets. Though every feature of the lady was indeed worthy of attention, I, with my regrettably conservative values, requested Alex to stop for a while so I could take a picture of the river. "I can't stop on the bridge. The police will catch us," said he, without taking his eye off the lady's back. It was not until the heavenly body swerved towards the Sheriff department store that Alex stepped on the accelerator. Every lamppost alternated with flags of Russia and Transnistria. On both sides of the road were a mind-boggling gathering of signs regulating vehicles and pedestrians.

Village settlements covered entire hillocks. On road to Transnistria.

The walnut-lined road to Transnistria

Bendery Fortress, originally built by Stefan cel Mare before being captured by Suleiman the Magnificent in 1538.

WAR CEMETERY, BENDER

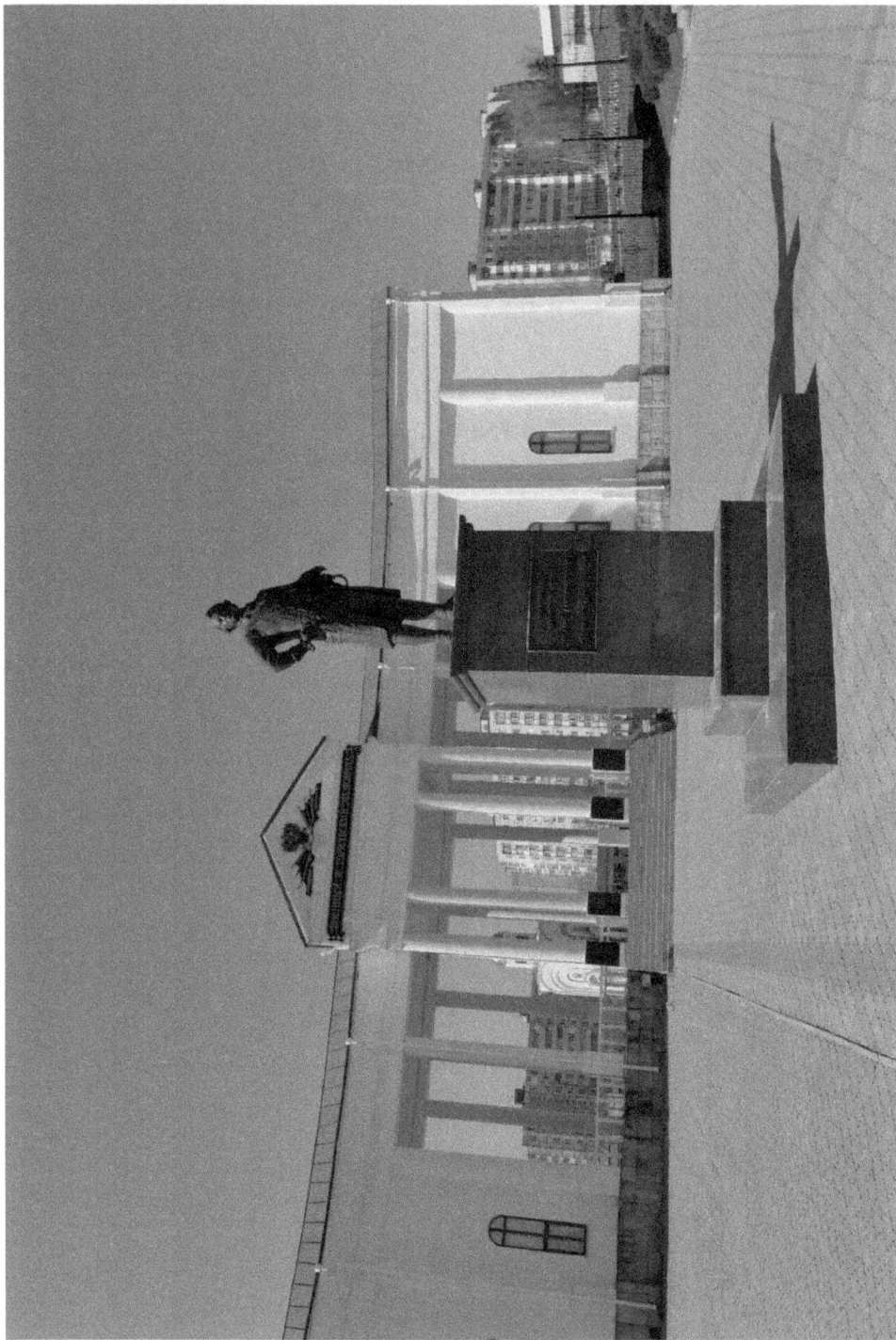

STATUE OF GENERAL POTEMKIN IN BENDER

Walls pockmarked with bullet holes show signs of savage combat during the Transnistria War. Bender.

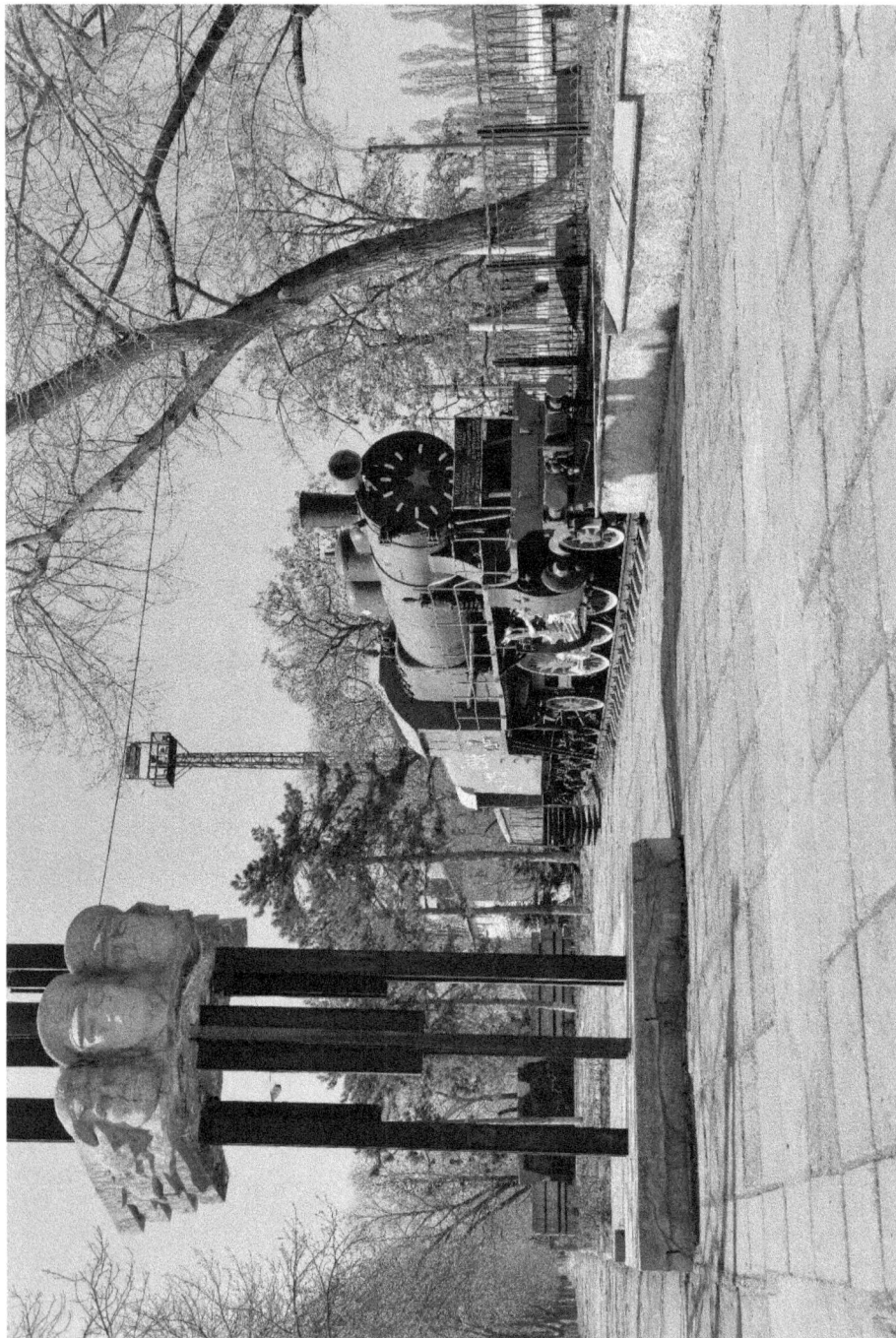

An old Russian CY 06-71 steam locomotive and the granite mural memorialising the rail workers who lost their lives during the 1917 Russian Revolution. Bender.

ГАРА ВОКЗАЛ

BENDER RAILWAY STATION

LENIN MONUMENT IN BENDER

In Tiraspol, Alex stopped at the viciously expansive building of the Transnistrian government or parliament, on the opposite side of the road. An imposing red granite statue of Vladimir Lenin, his coat tail flying in the breeze, loomed large in front of the building. "No, no! Don't step out to take a picture. Hurry! Give me your camera and I will quickly shoot. Police doesn't like people taking pictures of administrative buildings," whispered Alex. Moving his body away from the window, he clicked two badly framed pictures and drove away hoping he had not been spotted. The giant statue of Lenin continues to haunt citizens and terrorise tourists.

A few metres away was a war memorial stuffed with graves, and De Wollant Park that sprouted more busts of authors and poets than flowers. As soon as we had parked, I darted across the road, with Alex in tow, to see the equestrian statue of Field Marshal Alexander Suvorov, the last Generalissimo of the Russian Empire who crushed Poles, Turks and French, never lost a single major battle that he commanded, secured his country's far-flung borders, and was awarded the grandest titles by Russia and its allies for his great military deeds. He is judged by some military historians as a commander superior to Napoleon – and the man who founded Tiraspol. "That's the Russian story – that Suvorov established Tiraspol. Records show that it was a colony of the Greek city Miletus around 600BC. 'Tiras' was the Greek name for Dniester River," clarified Alex. Lonesome old ladies in head scarves sat on benches around the lofty sculpture.

Trotting back across the road, bypassing the war memorial, we went to the potholed pedestrian bridge across the Dniester to view the river. The ancient Greek name of Tiras is derived from the Scythian 'tura' – meaning 'rapid'. The river is anything but that – at least in Tiraspol. It flows sluggishly through the city, carrying only the reflections of the skeletal trees that line its course. Originating in Ukraine, the 1,362-km river traverses 398 km of Moldova before pouring into the Black Sea.

During the Neolithic period the valley of Dniester River was home to one of the most advanced civilisations of earth – the Cucuteni-Trypillia culture that existed between 5300 to 2600 BC. Abundant archaeological remains show that there was a proliferation of farming communities and the largest settlements in Europe with up to 45,000 inhabitants. For some unknown reason these settlements were demolished every 60-80 years – to be reconstructed many years later over the previous remains. My guess is that the farmers practiced slash-and-burn agriculture, shifting to greener pastures and returning to the burnt land once it was rejuvenated. Historically, Dniester has been a divisive waterway, serving as a boundary between countries. In antiquity, it divided Sarmatia and Dacia. From the 14th century to 1812, it formed the eastern boundary of the Principality of Moldova. Between the two world wars it marked the borders of Romania and USSR. Today, it divides Moldova and Transnistria.

Returning to the war memorial, we walked past a rugged Soviet T-34 tank, its canon pointing (almost) towards the Russian orthodox church, and past the tomb of the Unknown Soldier and the eternal flame. We loitered amongst the graves of the soldiers and bronze sculptures raised in the memory of those killed during the Soviet occupation (1979-89) of Afghanistan, and in the 1990-92 Transnistria War. These memorials ensure those killed in battles do not fall victims to history's forgetfulness.

We continued driving on 25 October Street, stopping in front of the city hall, the House of Soviets, a white Stalinist building, its front embellished with a black bust of a scowling Lenin raised on a red granite pedestal. As Lenin sculptures are fast becoming extinct, I got off to capture this bust with my camera. As a rebellious teenager, I had read several of Lenin's works and admired his revolutionary zeal, his organisational ability to unite the have-nots to overthrow the haves. As a student in Seattle, I had even pinned his metallic head on my denim jacket – not because of any leanings towards communism – but as an act of defiance against capitalism. My curiousity, not liking, in Marxism ideology led me into trouble with the US government. Someone has rightly said: "If at 18 you are not a communist, something is wrong with you. If at 30, you are still a communist – something is wrong with you." After having travelled to 119 countries (as on September 2018), including most of the countries that were once a part of USSR, I am convinced that the repressive communist system of governance did not promote happiness or a civilised society in which one could live without fear.

The clock on the House of Soviets stuck noon. "There is only one more thing of interest to see in Tiraspol –the Soviet MIG-19 monument," said Alex. It was already getting late and we still had to drive over 200 km to see the monasteries at OrheiVechi and Curchi in Moldova before returning to Chisinau. "Screw it!" said I. "Let's go to the Tourism Office to buy Transnistrian stamps and get the hell out of here." Transnistria is just a depressing Soviet relic, a living museum of communist times with decrepit and identical block houses; streets peppered with statues of Lenin and posters of Stalin; billboards celebrating past Russian triumphs; an intelligence agency still called KGB; streets named after Marx, Engels, Lenin and Felix Dzerzhinsky, the founder of the Soviet secret police; and big-hatted policemen and soldiers in Soviet uniforms harassing innocent pedestrians. It was a stifling atmosphere not suited to my liberal mind.

At Strada Sovietic, we stepped into the Transnistria Tourist Centre, a two-room office where I could pick up some souvenirs. A delicate lady with gentle blue eyes, an amiable voice and a graceful figure greeted me warmly. Her cheerful demeanour lightened my spirits. When she got to know I was from India, she excitedly said that I was Transnistria's first Indian guest. I gave her the benefit of the doubt. Locking her arm into mine, she got Alex to take pictures with her phone-camera to post on tourism office's Facebook page. I left Transnistria in good humour. The invisible immigration officer at the border even let me retain the exit coupon as a souvenir.

Lenin statue in front of Parliament House, Tiraspol

War Memorial, Tiraspol.

Memorial to soldiers killed in Afghanistan. Tiraspol.

Memorial to soldiers killed in Transnsitrian War (1990-92)

Dniester River in Tiraspol

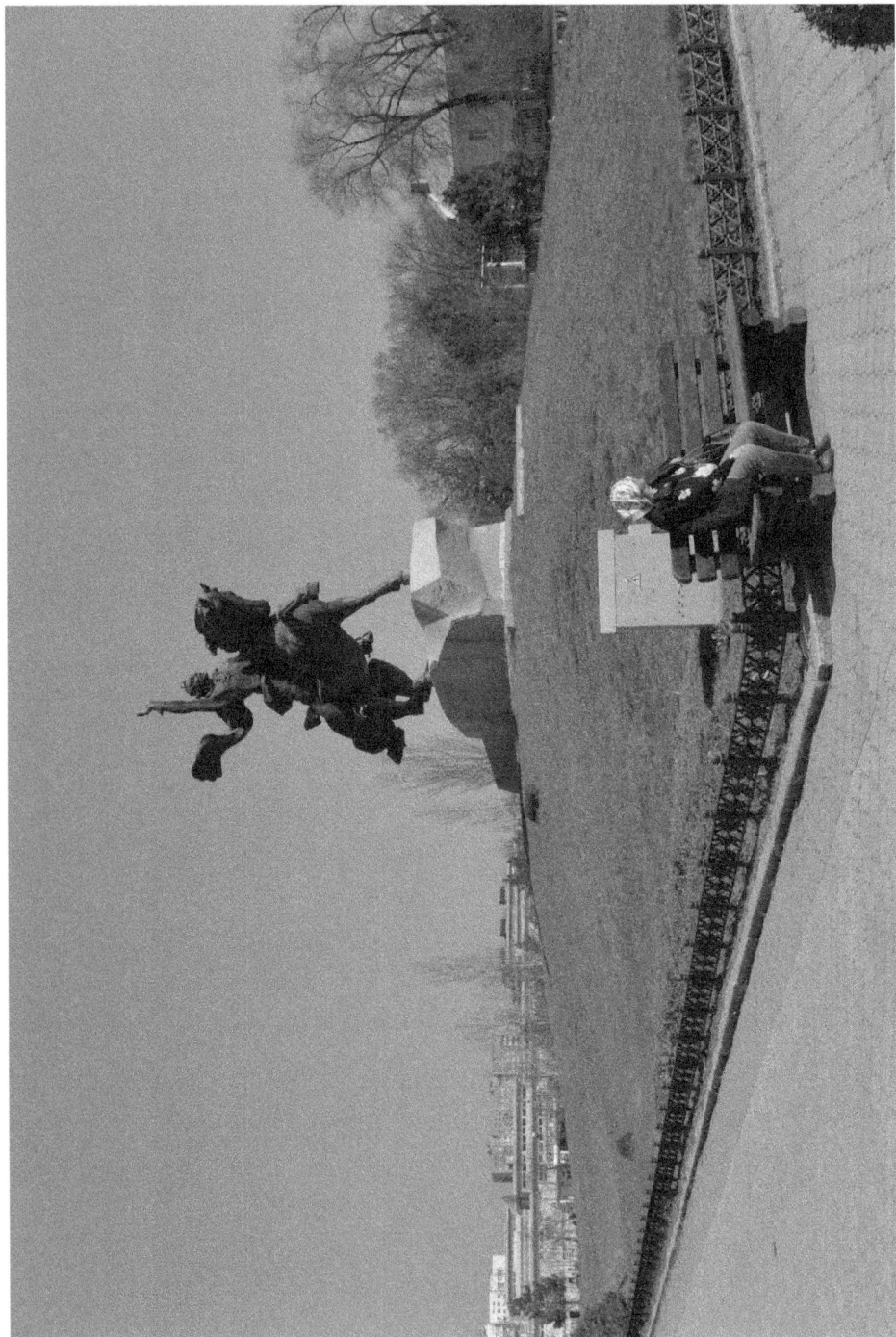

Statue of Field Marshal Alexander Suvorov in Tiraspol

Bust of a scowling Lenin in front of the House of Soviets in Tiraspol

The 92km distance to OrheiVechi was covered in two hours. We drove back towards Chisinau, past large village settlements that covered entire hillocks, modest houses with private vineyards and fields being ploughed by horses. Bypassing the city on a potholed road along an archaic thermal power plant we got on to R23 before turning right into a country road that winded through picturesque villages with blue-fronted houses bordered with stone walls. A sparkling stream fell from the forested mountainous heights and splashed into a rushing river.

Alex stopped at a viewpoint that provided a distant but spectacular sight of the new Orhei monastery. I clambered down the grassy mountainside and stood over an unfenced precipice gazing at the narrow valley and the long range of perpendicular cliffs rising across the silent, meandering Raut River, a tributary of Dniester. The solitary, diminutive monastery perched on the high cliffs, at the edge of the sky, looked like a sentinel eagle watching over the grand scenery.

A short distance later, we stopped to gaze at another enchanting spectacle of Trebujeni village deep down below. I was unable to tear my eyes from the heavenly vision. Alex announced it was time to leave and bundled me into the car. "This beautiful landscape is being considered by UNESCO as a World Heritage Site," remarked Alex.

The UNESCO website has this to say about the **OrheiulVechi Archaeological Landscape:**

"The Landscape comprising the territory of the Trebujeni and Butuceni villages,resembles a hemispherical amphitheatre...defined by the Răut's steep and high banks. The extremely tortuous course of the Răut, 15 to 20 meters wide, has carved embedded meanders, which together stretch for 7,000 meters, through limestone bedrock. The downstream left bank is nearly upright and reaches ca. 100-148 meters

in altitude. At the western and south-eastern ends of the escarpment, two natural passages, respectively 80 meters and 300 meters wide, link this naturally fortified central areas to the surrounding region.

The Landscape is dramatic and beautiful because of its highly unusual geomorphology, and it and its surroundings are rich in subsistence resources: chernozem soils that are enormously productive, meadows and forests rich in wild fruits and medicinal herbs, many springs of fresh water, varied aquatic and terrestrial fauna. At the same time, the area abounds in building materials: limestone, sand, clay and wood. The Landscape provides excellent natural defensive conditions, not just the natural escarpments, but also because it is at a generally higher elevation than the wide surrounding areas, while the Răut and its tributaries ensure the connection with the Black Sea, where maritime trade flourished since the 5th Millennium BC. These factors combine to render the landscape of OrheiulVechi very different from the rest of the region. That is why, since prehistoric times, humans in large numbers were attracted to the area. Therefore, the density of archaeological evidence is unusually high within the Landscape."

Descending to the river, we saw traces of ancient baths that testify to the existence of a vanished settlement. An extensive face of a cliff had a complex of tiered caves that could only be accessed by birds, mountain goats and monks. Arriving in Butuceni village, the vehicle crawled slowly over rocks. Both sides of the path were lined with small, modest houses that were in a primitive state.

Before climbing to the cave monastery, Alex suggested we have lunch at the Butuceni Eco Resort. Parking the car next to an ancient well sheltered by a wooden roof and encased in blue walls, we walked to the restaurant that was tastefully decorated in the old-fashioned way. Dried corn cobs adorned the walls of the veranda. Window sills were lined with little pots of flowers. It was past lunchtime and the staff, ladies dressed in quilted vests and embroidered caps, arranged and dusted the rugged wooden furniture with straw brooms. Terracotta mugs and glasses sat on the wood-fired oven. Cheap rugs covered the floor. Handlooms hung from a wall at one end of the room and a string of cane baskets filled with wool were placed before them. There were divans with lace sheets and stacks of fluffy pillows with embroidered covers of flowery designs. In this rustic ambience, Alex enjoyed his meatballs while I savoured Red Borsch, a soup made from beetroot, carrot, potato, cabbage, onion and pepper sauce. Still hungry, I ordered Cighiri, a local delicacy of debateable merit, made from minced meat of liver, heart, lard, egg, onion and garlic.

Under a baking sun and on full stomach, the steep 15-minute climb to the cave monastery seemed too undesirable a task. I asked Alex if it was possible to drive up to the cave. "Let's try," he said. I regretted my request. The car crawled up the mountainside, shuddering over rocks and vegetation, rocking and tilting precariously. My fingers were placed on the door handle, ready to bail out. If the vehicle didn't tumble, surely some part of the machine would snap. Now I was plagued with the fear that Alex would demand compensation from me for the repairs. What would be my arguments for not paying? How will I make it back to Chisinau? I was to fly to Kiev early next morning. At a point, where a sickly horse was tied to a wooden peg, Alex said he could go no further, and we would have to walk the rest of the way. Before he could finish the sentence, I was already on terra firma.

We strode into mouth of the 13th century cave monastery and tip-toed with arched backs through rocks as old as nature. A frail monk with a placid face, sunken blue eyes, a hoary grey beard and strings of dead hair falling from the sides of his bald head, sat motionless behind an ancient desk, holding his head in his hand as if he was hung-over. The cave opened into a spacious hall, its stone walls bedecked with icons and lit up with burning lamps. A lady, dressed in a black gown and a headscarf, dusted the sacred space and tended the lamps, talking in whispers to the monk who, in between his coughing spasms, would grunt a few words in a graveyard voice. With folded hands, I bent low to greet the monk and would have kissed his bony hands if I was not revolted by the sight of his long, dirty fingernails. On my request, Alex asked the sage if I could take a picture with him. He nodded his agreement. I threw my arm around his hunched back and he twisted his gums into a grin.

I wanted to ask the grizzled, age-defying monk the story of his life, and seek refreshment in his precious words. Was it a broken love affair, a distressed family life, that had driven him to the loneliness of monkhood and wilderness? Was he escaping justice for some grave crime he had committed? Did he have the power to bring down the stars from heaven, to make the moon tremble? What were the life's gravest mysteries that he had mastered? What were the bursts of inspiration he had received from practising austerities? But he seemed too downcast and tired to answer my queries - and I let him be. Holding the sides of the cliff we entered the dark recesses of an adjoining cavern where the languishing monks sought brightness and slept on rough rocks seeking ecstatic pleasure in excruciating pain.

Returning to the cave monastery, I stepped out on the breezy terrace that offered idyllic views. For countless years the monks of yore must have sat in this airy elevation, in between their meditations, to enjoy the beauty of the surroundings, a cup of wine in hand, gazing at the wooded hillsides, watching the swifts and swallows flitting in and out of their abodes in craggy cliffs; eyeing village girls herd cattle to the stream deep down below and plait their hair looking at their reflection in the brook's smooth waters. The primeval stillness would often be shattered by the howls of whirling storms and bolts of hellish lightning.

A short walk on the top of the ridge brought us to the new church built by the villagers in 1905 and dedicated to the Ascension of Mary. Shut down by the humourless Soviets in 1944, it remained abandoned during the communist period. A bunch of priests occupied the property in 1996 and restored it with public money. From the several donation boxes placed strategically in the complex, it seems that collecting funds continues to be their principal occupation. There were no bowing and scraping worshippers. Four pastors stood in a huddle under the shade of a tree. Gold and silver glittered on their gowns. The arrogance on their frowning but radiant faces, and in their strained movements, reflected that they were well adapted to the magnificence of power and fashion.

Back in the car, Alex inched forward on a narrow track left by the hooves of the village cattle till it disappeared into a channel filled with rainwater. Reversing was not an option. Alex got off to inspect the way forward, confirming that the soil would hold. Though I admired his cool-headedness, I entrusted myself to the will of God and the residing spirits of this power place. Skilfully manoeuvring the wheels over the edges of the pit, the car took an eternity to creep towards safety. As we descended, a coarse-clad farmer tramping wearily along,driving a loose cow, suddenly appeared in front of us. The cow was as surprised as we were. Turning around, it bolted, running ahead of the rattling car all the way down to the village.

"The solitary, diminutive monastery perched on the high cliffs, at the edge of the sky, looked like a sentinel eagle watching over the grand scenery." New Orhei Monastery.

Trebujeni Village

Trebujeni Village

Ancient baths outside Trebujeni

A restaurant decorated in the old-fashioned way. Buteceni Village.

An aspiring monk

Cave monastery in Orhei.

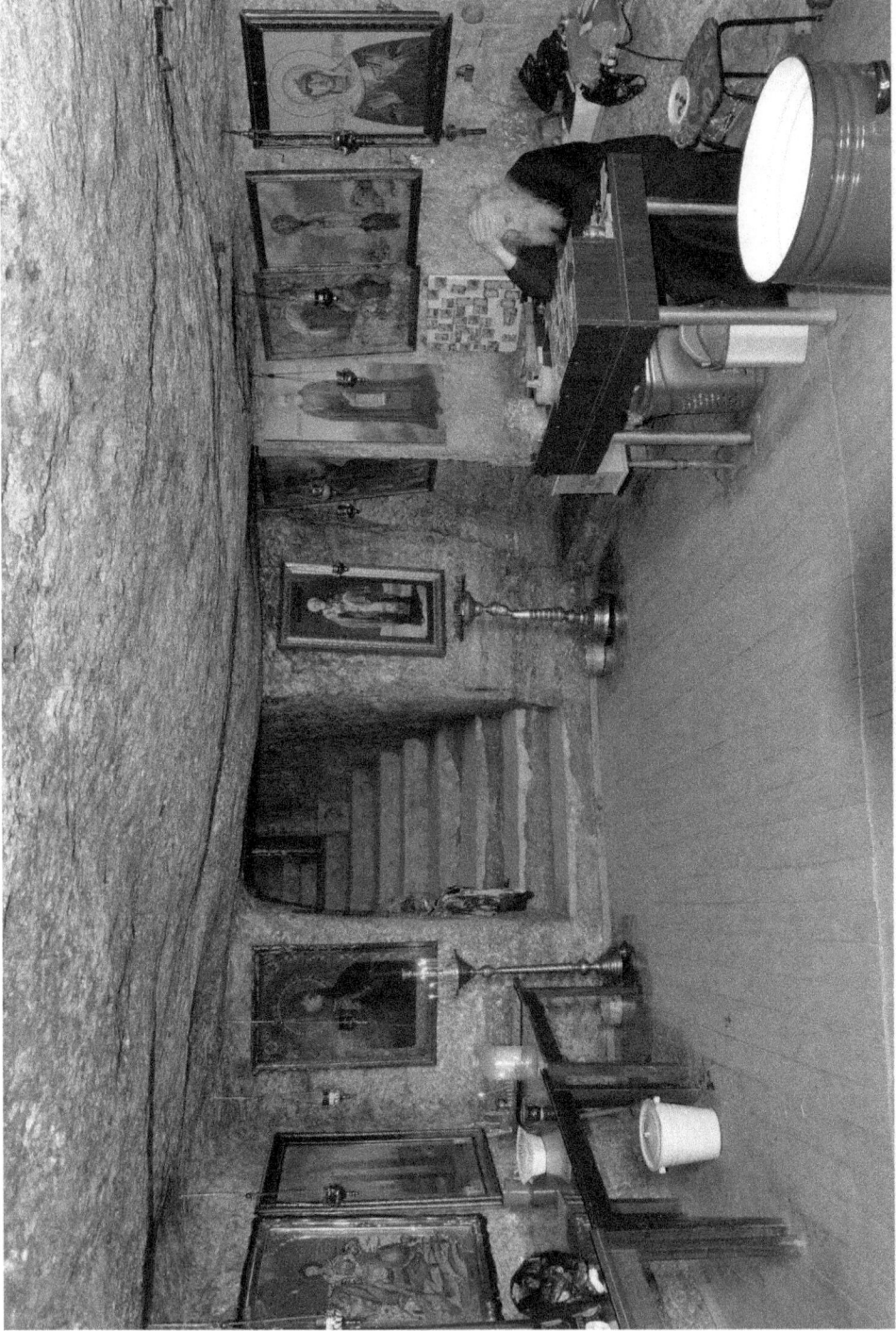

The "hungover" monk in cave monastery. Orhei.

View of Raut River from Orhei Cave Monastery

The new church dedicated to the Ascension of Mary. Orhei.

Interior of Ascension of Mary Church. Orhei.

The country road winded through picturesque villages with blue-fronted houses. Enroute Orhei.

Fourteen km southwest of Orhei, amongst a forest of codru trees, on the banks of Vatic River, lies the Curchi monastery, a gem of Bessarabian architecture, the richest, largest and most beautiful monastery in all of Moldova. "We have lost much of our forests," said Alex. "Lush codru forests covered 30 percent of our land. Now it is only 11 percent. Many robbers and thieves infested these forests. Moldova was known as the Land of Hajduks, of heroic outlaws who stole from the rich and gave to the poor." The monastery might have been founded by a robber.

According to one version of its history, DumitraşCurcă, a strong and powerful thug from the village of Morozeni in Orhei county, used to waylay people passing through the forest. Once, having murdered some travellers, he was shocked to find his parents among those killed. Deeply distraught and pained by his own gruesomeness, he sought God's forgiveness. A hermit from Rasca advised him to build a monastery from the money he had looted. He did as he was told - and the monastery was named in his "honour". Whether God pardoned him for his horrific acts, we do not know.

The most reliable version is that the monastery was built in 1773 by two brothers, Iordachi and Mihai Curca, to soothe their guilty conscience. The Tartars had been making frequent slave-raiding incursions into Bessarabia, terrorising the population. The two brothers, along with a priest and his two children, fled Buzesti village, where they lived. Several months later, the priest fell seriously ill. Lying on his deathbed, he confided to the brothers about the treasure he had buried in their village and requested them to retrieve it and use the money for the welfare of his children. As soon as the brothers had performed the last rites of the priest, they returned home with the two children. The Tartars were still occupying the village. They caught Iordachi and prepared to kill him. But he talked his way out, trading the two children for his own freedom. The brothers again left the village. Many months later, after the Tartars had withdrawn, they came back to find the village plundered and razed. Though they took possession of the treasure, they were filled with remorse for having abandoned the children and betrayed the priest's trust. To atone for their sin, they used their ill-gotten wealth to build a wooden church at the spot where they found the treasure. The brothers also became monks – taking the names of Joan and Manasie.

Over the years, the monastery added land and structures and grew into a fine architectural ensemble of five churches, hermitage and other buildings – like wine cellars and strongholds – required to keep the priests in comfort and safety. Extensive orchards produced fruits to make quality wines. Curchi gained wealth and fame – until the Soviets kicked out all the priests, burnt over 4,000 holy books, destroyed numerous icons and turned the place into a psychiatric hospital. In 1999, when renovation began, there were still corpses lying inside one of the churches that had been converted into a morgue.

Parking the car in the vacant lot, Alex, stroking his stomach, walked away to answer the call of nature. I walked past two scowling, armed soldiers posted outside the bell tower that also served as the monastery gate. Inside the compound, everything was exquisite. The stone walls were inlaid with gilded mosaics of saints and crosses. The two-tiered garden was splendidly landscaped with carpets of grass, spindly trees, verdant bushes, gravel tracks and snow-white fountains. Amidst them all stood the two principal churches, their domes sprouting golden crosses. I tottered through both, blinded by the opulence of the glittering golden wall of the iconostasis, the brilliant icons, the dome and the walls splashed with colourful frescoes – everything following the lavish pattern of the Orthodox churches. The fund-raising campaign of

2006, *"Curchi Monastery: From Ruins to Elevation"*, has been successful in restoring the monastery to its pristine glory.

I was the only tourist in the sacred fortress. In the Church of the Nativity of the Mother of God, a Moldavian couple was enjoying a private moment while their toddler crawled joyously on the marble-tiled floor. Outside, I came across some priests as grave and stern as the guarding soldiers. Some sat joyously with nuns on a low wall, swinging their legs and indulging in whispered conversations that didn't seem to be on religious issues.

In a setting sun, we drove into Chisinau, 55 km from Curchi. Alex, tired after a long day of driving, was anxious to get back to his wife and kids. Lightly enlightened after visiting the monasteries, I desired to have the favourite food of priests: bunnies. Alex recommended Penthouse, across the street from the hotel, in Stefan cel Mare Park.

"Penthouse? I am not looking for Playboy bunnies. Just want to eat the regular rabbit," said I, laughing.

"Of course. They have the best," reassured Alex.

A sucker for tradition, I first had the *Zeama*, a "traditional Moldovan soup" with God-knows-what contents and an outmoded taste, before ordering the main course: *Iepure In Sos De Frisca Cu CartofiCopti,* braised rabbit with baked potatoes. The top floor of the two-storied restaurant was not too busy, and the staff was watching a Russian TV channel. The young waiter, assigned to my table, seeing an opportunity to practice his English, engaged me in a conversation. He turned out to be a theology student.

"You want to be a priest?" I asked.

"No. I will teach people who want to become priests. That's better."

"With the Soviets gone, I am sure religion will now be a growth industry."

"Indeed. Only I.T. might do better."

I could not resist asking him about the fondness of Christian priests for rabbit meat.

In Mesopotamia, since pre-Christian times, hare or rabbit has been a symbol of vitality, sexual desire and fertility – which also signifies rebirth and resurrection. In Greco-Roman world, rabbits were depicted on gravestones. Early Christians followed this practice. Hence, Easter bunny's association with the resurrection of Christ.

Catholics, it is said, breed like rabbits. Even Pope Francis says so. In an inflight interview from Manila to Rome, he famously said: "**Some think that — excuse the language — to be good Catholics, we have to be like rabbits.**" In Poland, with 87 percent Catholic population, the government is encouraging citizens to "breed like rabbits". It has invested over $600,000 in a 30-second video ad featuring bunnies happily munching lettuce and carrots while a rabbit raconteur discloses the secret of producing many offspring – exercising, avoiding stress and having a healthy lifestyle. The ad ends with a young couple enjoying a romantic picnic.What accounts for the celibate monks love for rabbit that is associated with unfettered lust and sexual excess? The theology student had an answer.

"During Lent, the 40-day period before Easter when Christians give up good things as a form of penance, they were forbidden to eat meat on Fridays. In 600 AD, the considerate Pope Gregory declared that it was okay for people to eat only one kind of meat during Lent: baby rabbits. They were not considered meat. That's how priests and other people started domesticating rabbits. That's the story I have heard," he explained, with a smirk.

Returning to the kitchen, he came back with the rabbit meat covered with white sauce. "Ah! I have thought of another reason why priests like to eat rabbits. Because, before they eat, the rabbits say: 'Lettuce pray'." He had to explain the joke to elicit my laughter. While I nibbled at the meat, images of Bugs Bunny and the gentle, white, furry creatures hopping around, drifted through my mind, ruining my appetite.

Early next morning, I flew out of Chisinau to Kiev, leaving behind the good people of Moldova, seasoned hostages to geopolitical games, to figure out why, after 200 years of Russian management and 50 years of Soviet "modernising", they are still the poorest in Europe; if they should give up on Transnistria as a nightmare, realise the Romanian dreams of reunion or stay independent and join the European Union. Once these grave issues are settled, I would love to return to Moldova and spend a scandalous year or two like the frivolous Pushkin beforeretiringhurt to the lonely grandeur of the cave monastery at Orhei to fantasise away my old age. By all accounts, Moldovans are wavering and vacillating. They could take generations to decide on these matters. They can take all their time. I am in no hurry. As a Hindu, I will be reborn as a punishment for the sins I have committed. I have no desire to attain moksha, to liberate myself from the cycle of birth and death. I shall continue sinning to ensure that I am reborn – in Moldova, perhaps. And I promise not to ditch the country by migrating to greener pastures.

"The stone walls were inlaid with gilded mosaics of saints and crosses." Curchi Monastery.

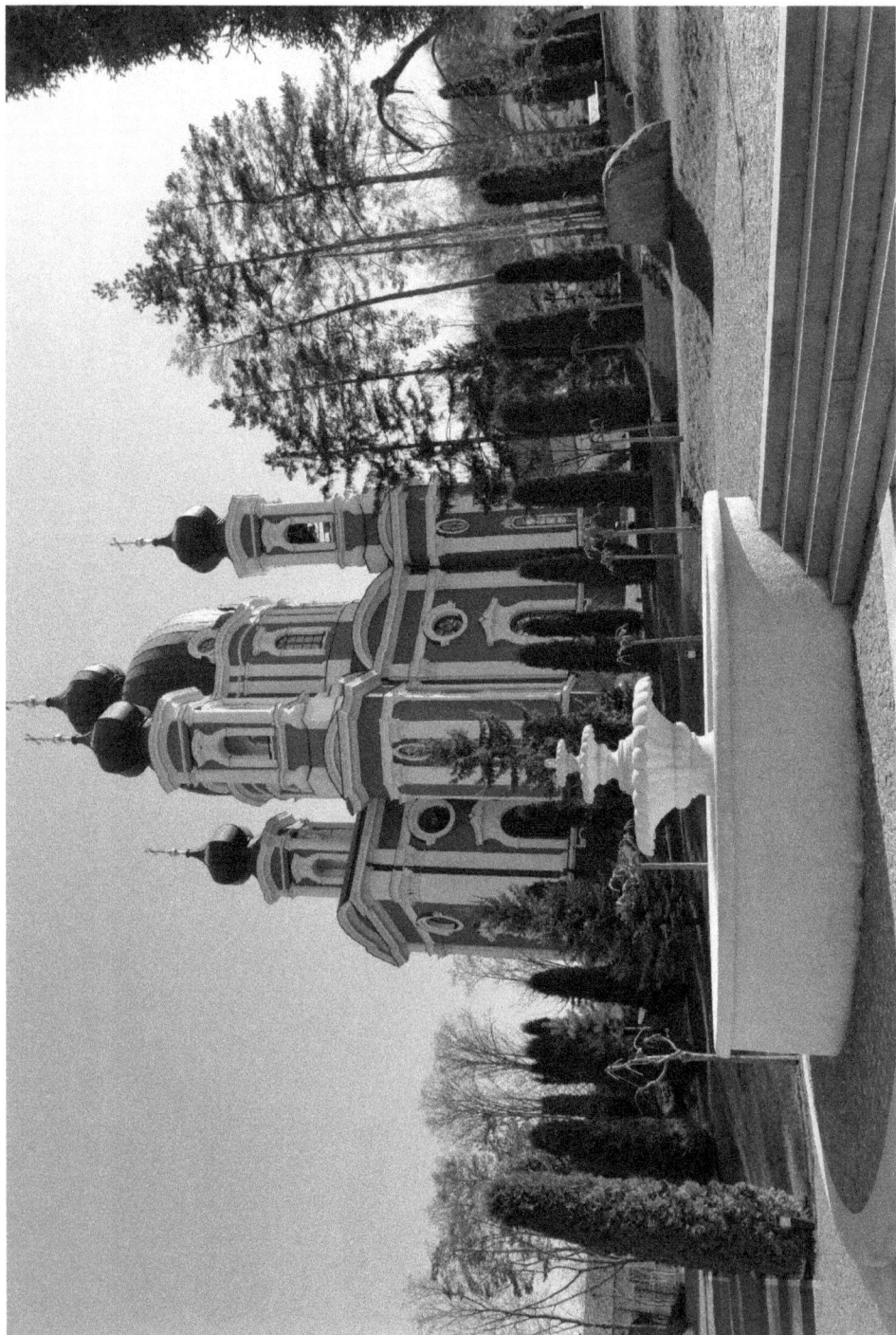

Church of the Nativity of the Mother of God. Curchi.

Interior of Eastern Orthodox Church. Curchi.

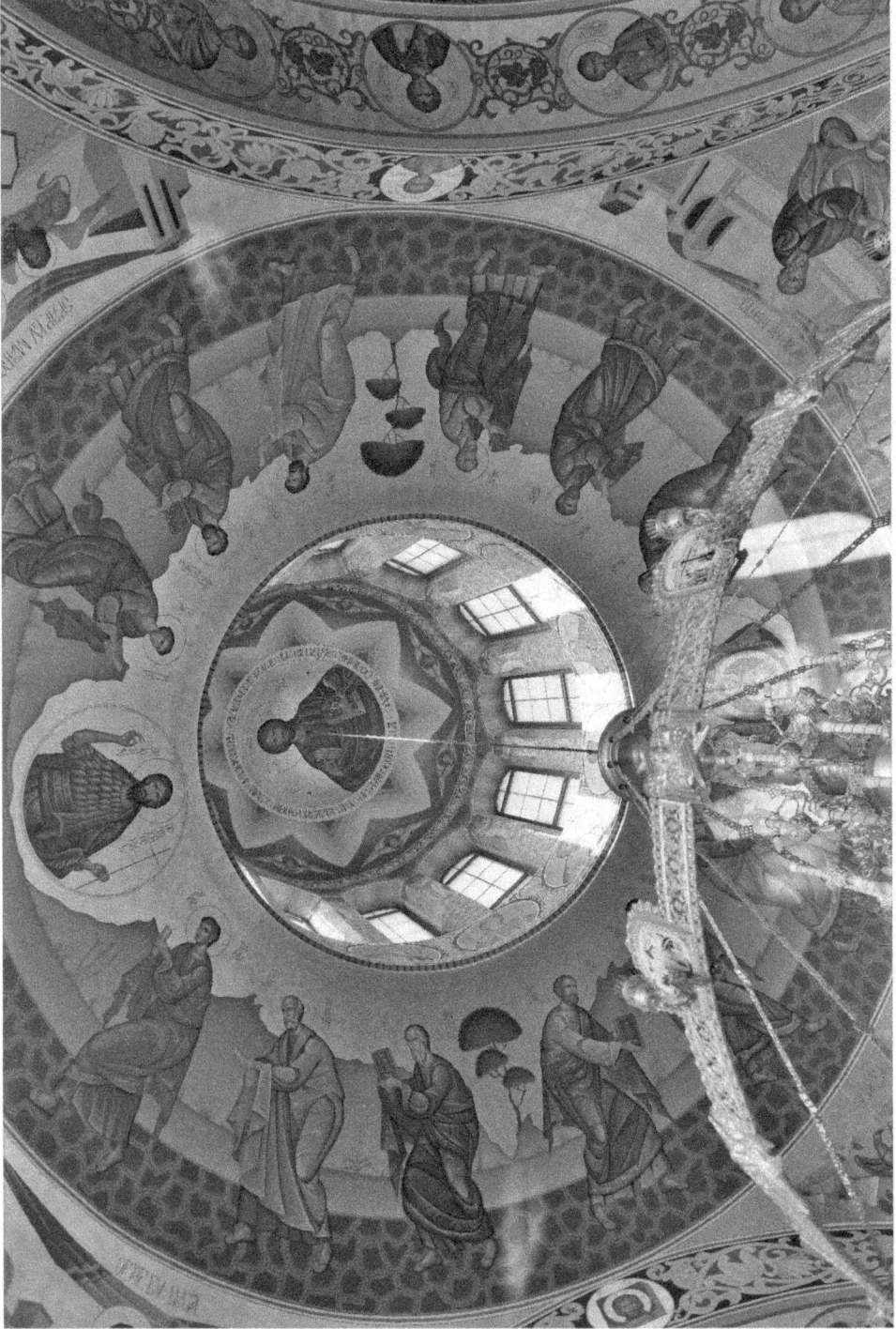

Dome of Eastern Orthodox Church. Curchi.

The dome and walls of the Eastern Orthodox Church splashed with colourful frescoes.

The blinding opulence of the glittering golden wall of the iconostasis in the Church of the Nativity of the Mother of God. Curchi.

The Church of the Nativity of the Mother of God. Curchi.

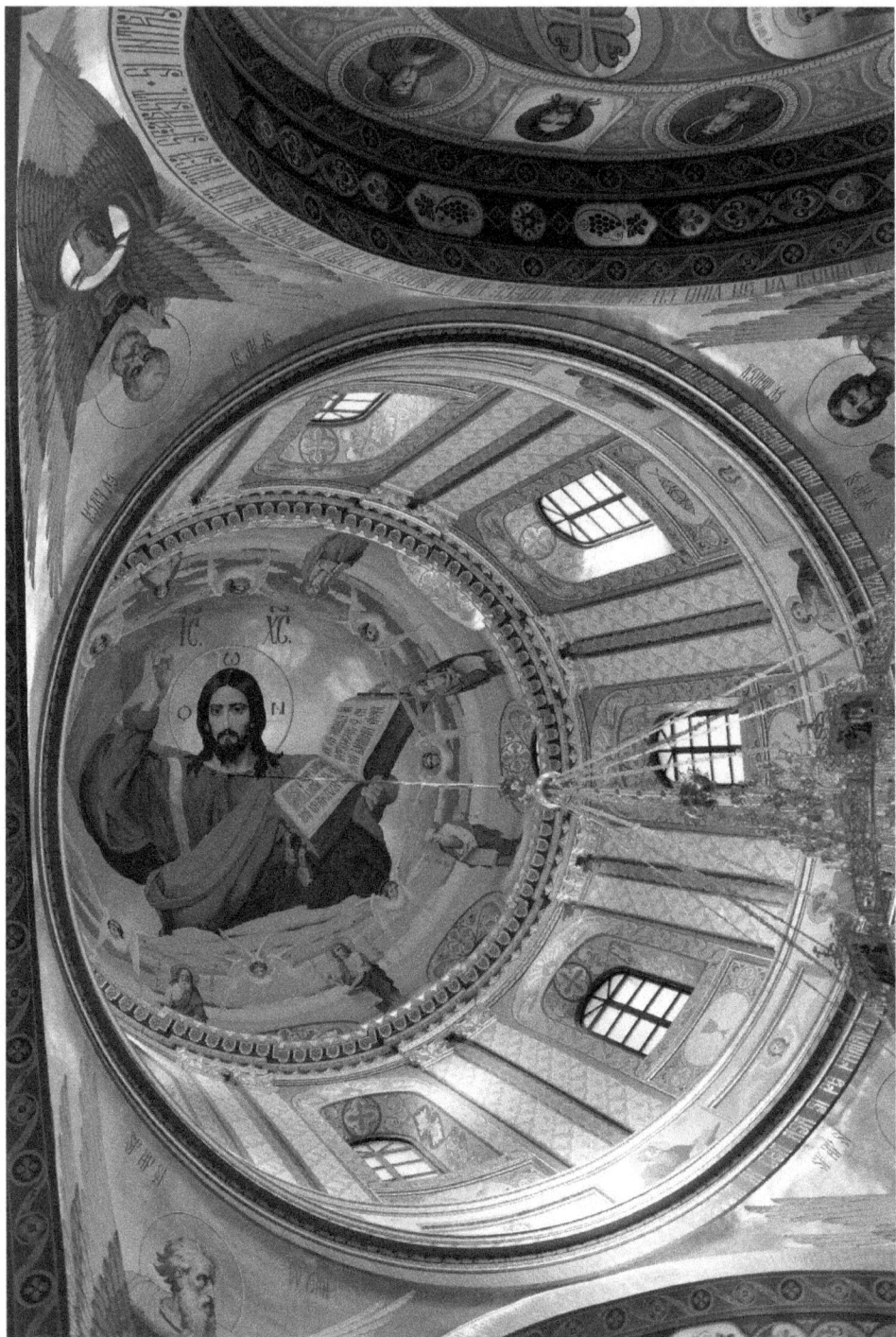

Dome of the Church of the Nativity of the Mother of God. Curchi.

Church of the Nativity of the Mother of God. Curchi.

Other Books by Akhil Bakshi

Printed Books

Arctic to Antarctic: A Journey Across the Americas

Back to Gondwanaland – Travels through West Asia and Africa

Between Heaven and Hell – Travels through South Asia

The Road to Freedom – Travels through Singapore, Malaysia, Burma and India

I'll Follow the Sun – Travels to Here, There, Everywhere

Silk Road on Wheels – Travels through Central Asia, Chinese Turkestan and Tibet

Gondwanaland Expedition – coffee table book

Askar Akaev: A Political Journey

E-Books – available on Amazon Kindle

In the Heart of America: Travels in Mexico and Central America

Autumn in Alaska

Arctic to Antarctic: A Journey Across the Americas

Explorations in Tierra del Fuego

Cradle of Civilization: Travels in Peru

Magic of Bolivia

Spirit of Colombia

66° North: Travels in Iceland

Afghanistan: An Empire of Blood and Ash

Berlin: A Walk through History

Silenced Buddha – Travels in Sri Lanka

Golden Swamp – Travels in Bangladesh

Ireland: Wild and Furious

Kumbh Mela: Faith and Hypocrisy

Ruins of Angkor

Rum, Reggae and Columbus: Cruising the Caribbean

Skytrain to Lhasa

Stairway to Heaven – Circumambulation of Mt. Kailash in Tibet

Down Dalton Highway

www.ingramcontent.com/pod-product-compliance
Lightning Source LLC
Chambersburg PA
CBHW032042040426
42449CB00007B/984